the power of

parent-child play

the power of parent-child play

LAURIE WINSLOW SARGENT

Tyndale House Publishers, Inc.
Wheaton, Illinois

Library of Congress Cataloging-in-Publication Data

Sargent, Laurie Winslow.
   The power of parent-child play / Laurie Winslow Sargent.
     p. cm.
Includes bibliographical references (p. 231) and index.
ISBN 0-8423-5764-5
1. Play. 2. Parent and child. 3. Parenting. 4. Child rearing. I. Title.
HQ782 .S34 2003
306.874—dc21   2002014263

Printed in the United States of America

08   07   06   05   04   03
5   4   3   2   1

To my darling, creative, supportive husband, Gordy.
May we enjoy playing together for yet *another*
twenty-five years—or more!

Special thanks to so *many* people in my life who have nurtured me as a mother and a writer since I began my adventures in both professions. Were I to name you all, this would be a chapter, not a page!

To my family, from my lovely children and husband and extended family, to my gracious, merciful Father in heaven. I marvel at the unwavering support and encouragement I've felt from you *all!* I know that not all writers have it so good.

To my many dear friends, but in particular Cyndi Moor Jones. For nearly twenty-five years you have made me laugh, made me think, and nurtured me through countless ups and downs in life.

To my many inspiring colleagues: my agents (i.e., my cheerleaders) at Alive Communications, my sensitive and wise editors at various publications who have helped teach me how to edit myself better, and fellow writers I've met through NCWA and inspiring writers' conferences. Thanks to Johnna Howell, Judy Bodmer, Thornton Ford, Paul Malm, and Barbara Koshar for your honest, dedicated critiques. You helped me revise and enhance this book until the words on the pages more clearly began to reflect what I hope to convey with my heart.

To my fellow parents in various moms' groups, including Moms in Touch—moms with whom I've rejoiced and commiserated for over five years.

Finally, thanks to all of you who were willing to share your play struggles with me and the readers of this book. I believe your words will encourage other mothers and fathers as they try new ways to play with their children.

Introduction
Parent-child play does not come
easily to all parents at all times!

Part 1: Play Benefits and Barriers

Part 2: Identifying and Overcoming Struggles

table of contents

Introduction

Parent-child play does not come easily

to all parents at all times!

t's a myth that playing with kids is always easy. In fact (children, avert your eyes) it can often be exasperating, messy, boring, or exhausting—even for the most loving parents. Gasp! Can a parent actually admit that?

Parenting has the potential to be extremely rewarding and joy producing. Yet various barriers prevent us from taking time to play with our children; others interfere with our ability to enjoy it fully. This book explores play struggles, and offers encouragement, solutions, and a good dose of humor. You'll read about how to:

- ⑨ Allow for personality differences—while keeping those differences from turning playtimes into battles. (What do you do when a perfectionistic or competitive child overturns a table game in anger?)
- ⑨ Choose activities that match your children's developmental needs and abilities.
- ⑨ Know what skills to look for so you don't miss exciting milestones.
- ⑨ Simplify play and have more fun by avoiding activities that are too expensive, messy, or time consuming to be worth the trouble.
- ⑨ Balance your time between necessary activities and intimate one-on-one play with one or more children.

- ☺ Help a dependent or social child find a balance between independent play and Mommy or Daddy time.
- ☺ Help your kids learn to take care of themselves and help with family chores in order to free up time for play.
- ☺ Make disciplining easier and decrease whining and defiance by integrating play into your lives.
- ☺ Keep sibling fighting from destroying a potentially fun family playtime.
- ☺ Find the best toys and games, and learn to use them in ways that fit your family.
- ☺ Balance quiet play at home with getting out and about. Turn family vacations into family adventures full of exciting and fond memories.
- ☺ Find new ways to have a *blast* with your kids!

Instead of guilting you into playing because it's good for your kids, I hope to persuade you to play because it's good for *you,* too. If you become more enthusiastic about play and more eager to spend one-on-one time with your children, they will naturally benefit as well.

Most of the chapters in this book begin with a story, followed by deeper exploration of specific barriers to play, then concrete ways you can make play work for you. You'll also find Questions for Reflection for each chapter (see appendix), which can be used for personal contemplation, journaling, or parent-support-group discussions.

Each chapter also includes Five-Minute Fun activities that require zero to few materials—and only five minutes to plan or do. (Feel free to play them longer, however!) If some activities are familiar to you, ask yourself, *Have I tried this game with this particular child? How long ago*?

Instead of merely giving you a list of activities, I hope to help you develop more of a play attitude—and a more playful spirit!

OPENNESS, VULNERABILITY, AND SACRIFICE

Twelve years ago, I was playing with my first child (then four years old) when a discouraged parent asked me, "How do you know how to play with your kid like that? How is it that you have so much fun together?"

I found those questions thought-provoking. Since then, I've been fascinated by the topic of play—reading what experts have to say about it and interviewing other parents to find out how *they* feel about it. That means my three children have grown up in a living laboratory. They have been raised by a mom who is probably more introspective about play than the average parent—one inclined to jump up during a game of UNO to jot down personal successes and failures.

Within these pages you will find the good, the bad, and sometimes the ugly—often within stories about my own family. That has required some vulnerability on my children's part. My kids are remarkable people. I desperately want to do them justice within these pages. Consequently, I've asked them to preview stories that don't put them in a favorable light, even temporarily. They've been amazingly supportive.

Yet, supporting this mission has not always been easy for them. One of our standing household jokes has been: "Mom can't play right now; she's too busy writing a book on play!" Balancing deadlines with family time has been a challenge. While writing about memories of past playtimes, I've feared I might miss the creation of new ones. My advice on overcoming time and energy barriers comes to you from the trenches.

Every single day I've been a parent, at least one child has made me laugh or touched my heart in some way. I would have missed many of those moments had I not taken time to play—to stop, look, and listen to my kids. By listening, I often hear very insightful or thought-provoking comments from children; I will share many of these with you. Don't let the fiction-style dialogue fool you into thinking I made any of it up! Kids can be amazingly insightful and funny.

Since the stories are topical rather than chronological, it may help you to know the current ages of the cast of characters in the Sargent family dramas. (You'd call a three-year-old's tantrum in a mall a drama, wouldn't you?)

Tyler, now sixteen, is an intelligent, determined, handsome young man who is looking at college brochures. Aimee, nearly twelve, is a sensitive, caring, lovely tween-ager just entering junior high—beginning the transition (sigh) from Beanie Babies to blush. Elisa, at five and a half, is a kindergartener full of that energy and enthusiasm most parents would love to bottle and sell—or use ourselves.

With four and a half years between the first two kids, and six between the last two, I've had many opportunities to play with my children together. It's also been a challenge at times to juggle all their needs separately. Other moms I interviewed for this book have children spaced very closely together. Whatever the spacing, the more kids, the more challenging parenting can be.

Yet there are ways to enjoy all of your children. My children—*your* children—will soon be grown and gone. By breaking through play barriers, we can all find ways to create memories of fun-filled, meaningful playtimes, build strong relationships with our children, and increase joy in our lives.

part 1
play
benefits
and barriers

chapter 1

one-size-fits-all?

The Variety of Ways to Play

It's so easy to miss out on joyful, rewarding playtimes with children when they're small, a time we can't recapture. You can play with your children in so many fun ways—perhaps more than you realize.

Ugh. What a disaster area. Dirty dishes, cereal boxes, and piles of papers. And cleaning the kitchen wasn't the only to-do item on my list. Let's see, balance checkbook, call my son's elementary school teacher . . .

"Mommy, come play with me." Four-year-old, three-foot-high Aimee pulled on my shirt.

"Oh, honey, I can't right now. Just look at this mess."

"Pleeeze?" Her high, squeaky voice edged into the whiny zone.

"Okay, okay. Um, how about if I set the oven timer for fifteen minutes from now. When it buzzes, I'll take a little coffee break with you, okay?"

I cleaned like a maniac, yet when the buzzer rang it was hard to stop. "Just one more counter to wipe, honey, and oh, let me put these bills away. Uh-oh. Is that one due already?"

"Mom, you promised."

Choosing between being an unkempt housekeeper or a promise-breaking mom, I opted for the former. But I set the timer again for ten more minutes. Let the buzzer be the bad guy, making me go back to work.

I sat on Aimee's carpet, mug in my hand. She said, oh-so-proudly, "I made you lunch!" and served me a plastic apple and a hot dog on a pink plastic dish. (No one told me when I became a mother how much plastic food I would eventually eat.)

"Mmmm, this is delicious," I said, while thinking, *Oops, I've got to return Gordy's shirt. . . . I wonder where the receipt went?* I nearly jumped to my feet to look for it. Then I remembered I was supposed to be playing.

"Here, Mommy, here's a cookie. I just baked it!" Aimee opened my palm and pretended to set something in it.

"Ohhh," I said. "A pretend one?"

"No," she said. "Not pretend, imaginary."

What? She finally had my attention. "Uh, what's the difference between pretend and imaginary?"

Aimee rolled her blue eyes a bit impatiently. Then her words rushed out: "Mom, you know. Pretend is when we say something is real, when it's not. Imaginary is when you can't, it's when you can't . . ." (she took a breath) "*see* it, but you *say* it's real." I smiled at the way she stuttered entire phrases in her eagerness to express herself, a little like tripping when you run too fast in flip-flops. Then it hit me.

"Oh! You mean the invisible cookie you just put in my hand is imaginary. But the plastic hot dog is pretend?"

She nodded.

Wow, I thought. *I've never once thought of pretend and imaginary as having different meanings. Do they really? Did she hear that somewhere or come to that conclusion on her own? Fascinating.*

Aimee poked at my empty palm. "See the green and red sprinkles on it?"

Suddenly her imagination took over mine. I could almost *see* those sprinkles. I became mesmerized by the way she pronounced her words, the way her long eyelashes batted gently. Suddenly all I could see and hear was my Aimee. Love for her overwhelmed me. My heart hurt, a genuine pain squeezing my breast, at the realization she would be four for so short a time.

Suddenly she jumped on me and hugged me. "Mommy, I love you so so *so* much."

Bzzzzzzzzzz. Darn that buzzer.

Years later, recalling that moment still chokes me up. Aimee, now eleven, paints her toenails blue and peppers her sentences with "like," as in, "You know, like, that guy, who was, like, on that show?" She still giggles when I tickle her. But instead of offering me plastic food, she's becoming more like her brother, whose idea of parent-child play is having Mom drive him to the mall.

Connecting with your child, even in short ten-minute bursts, is what helps make parenting so rewarding. But life so often gets in the way. If Aimee hadn't asked me to play that day, I might not have taken the time. And as you can see, even ten minutes can be powerful. I think we, as parents, need frequent reminders to stop and play, lest we miss out on those rewards.

DEFINING PLAY

Quite a few parents have asked me, "What qualifies as play?" as if there were one answer. Does sitting on the floor, coffee cup in hand, simply looking at a child and responding to her thoughts qualify? Absolutely. So do a host of other activities.

One dictionary defines the word *playful* as "high spirits, gaiety, and humor in action or speech."[1]

Hmmm. Fun seems to be one key element here. Do you have fun with your children? Do they have fun with you? And *how* do you do that? Let's look at intriguing synonyms for play found in *Webster's New World Thesaurus*[2]:

"Cut up, be the life of the party, play the fool, carry on."

Playing the fool may be tough for you if you struggle with spontaneity. Yet it can be learned, and I believe it is worth learning. You don't have to truly be a fool, but you can be willing to look a little silly on occasion in order to connect with others in a fun way. Silliness comes easier if you start with babies. Merely sticking a shoe on your head makes a baby laugh, because he's learned just enough about the way the world works to know that sneakers make ridiculous hats.

One evening when Tyler was six months old, he was trying so hard to crawl but just couldn't get it. Instead, he flopped about like a fish out of water. So—impulsively—I threw myself to the floor, copying his weird crawling attempts. I asked him, "Is *this* how you do it?" And that little six-month-old baby began to belly laugh hysterically. He was literally holding his little gut, gasping for air between giggles. Gordy heard his baby's laughter from the other room and insisted that I do the Fish Flop again, in front of him.

Well, as a mother, you can't sink much lower than flopping about on the carpet on your belly. But I was destined for silliness from that point on, doing anything it took to get a giggle from a child—a lovely, musical sound. And yes, my husband still respects me.

The synonyms for fun continue:

> *"To amuse oneself, make merry, play games, rejoice, have a good time, horse around."*

A game can be as simple as peekaboo with a baby, or as complex as a game of Risk or Monopoly with a teenager. But don't think that the word *games* must mean baby games, table or card games, or even the use of toys or crafts.

Some of my kids' favorite games require about a minute and revolve entirely around mundane chores—vacuuming, for instance. As I mow the carpet, my Vacuum Monster says, "Growl, growl, I am *so* hungry today; some little girls would be mighty tasty!" Then occasionally—without warning—I chase giggly preschoolers with the vacuum. They shriek delightedly, jumping up on the furniture. If the monster loses interest, the girls beg to be eaten again.

Another favorite, for little people as well as big people, usually occurs when my family is lazily lying around watching TV. I suddenly yell out, "Warm Laundry Alert!" and as they respond, "Oohh, me! Me!" I sprinkle warm T-shirts over them, fresh from the dryer.

As for horsing around, many dads identify with *that* definition of play. My husband's idea of tucking the kids in bed is jumping on them and wrestling with them. It's not highly conducive to sleep (ahem!) yet definitely conducive to giggles. Our friend Chuck makes kids into pillow sandwiches. He smashes a kid between two slices of bread (the pillows) after spreading on the condiments, a process which usually tickles.

"To frisk, cavort, dance, romp, frolic, skip, caper."

Many of my own family's favorite ways to play involve music: slow dancing with an infant, swing dancing with a four-year-old, rapping with a teen—just enough to make him grimace. I'm grateful for twenty-five years of marriage to a man who loves a wide variety of music: classical, jazz, scat, gospel, rock, and ethnic. He's my resident disc jockey.

One evening, while listening to music as we ate dinner, Gordy leapt from his seat, midbite. Turning up the stereo, he began conducting with a fork. Aimee and I left the table to jitterbug. Tyler donned dark glasses and lip-synched into a carrot. Five minutes later we were back to eating—but that little bit of goofiness had pulled our family together.

Even when we're immobilized by seat belts in the car, if the tunes are catchy enough, we revert to head dancing and disco-style finger-pointing. Sometimes I'll turn my kids' heads, arms, and legs into a drum set to keep the beat. Mixed with silly play are also tender moments, including dedicating songs to each other. Who can resist a six-foot-one mustached bodybuilder who lip-synchs to his fourth-grade daughter, "I'll be there, for better or worse, 'til death do us part, I love you with every beat of my heart."[3] Okay, put away the hanky and let's move on.

Here are a few more play definitions:

"Recreate, liberty, action" (hike or swim); "act in a play: impersonate" (eat imaginary cookies and play with

> *puppets); and "engage in a sport: participate, engage, rival, compete" (play tennis or shoot hoops).*

What a variety of ways there are to play! Play activities generally seem to fall into these categories (you may think of more):

- Silly, spontaneous, one-to-one play and silly family play
- Focused play: games, projects, playing with toys in a constructive way
- Focused family outings: to the zoo, library, sports activities, etc.
- Family vacations
- Calming, cuddly activities: reading, massage

By ridding yourself of preconceived notions about "real" play, you've already taken the first step toward eliminating barriers to play. Some parents feel guilty about never doing craft projects with their kids. Don't good parents do that? Not necessarily. Some prefer the great outdoors; others would rather snuggle in a rocking chair, reading *Winnie-The-Pooh*. Your own interests and style will cause you to play in your unique way.

Of course, it is healthy to stretch yourself occasionally. It may require more discipline for you to arrange a play date that's fun for your child yet less fun for you. If she loves arts and crafts and you hate them, making a project together can be a lovely gift to your child. You might not have fun completing the project, but you will find joy as you watch your child reach mental or motor milestones in the course of play.

What if your child's interests turn you off? By participating in these activities occasionally, you may find your own interest stimulated after all. I experienced this when Tyler was young. He had a penchant for collecting little black salamanders from a nearby creek. Ugh. Slimy little things. I truly disliked them.

However, as we learned more about them from library books and observed one as a pet, I gradually caught Tyler's interest. When Tyler was at school, I actually found myself surreptitiously visiting "Sally" in the aquarium in the laundry room and crooning at the little black thing. When Sally was sent to an untimely death as a result of its home being shaken from the gyrating washing machine, I was actually a little sad.

We have lasting memories of Sally, however: photos of the salamander crawling through a Lego maze, and a home video that still makes us laugh. In the video, three-year-old Aimee is exuberantly petting the creature, confidently describing how Sally loves to eat pancakes with syrup and play with her dolls. "Wookit his gween teef," *(teeth!?)* she exclaims, then she chatters on, absentmindedly stroking—no, *stretching*—the salamander's legs.

She suddenly pauses—at the precise moment we planned to intervene to prevent loss of limb—looks adoringly at Sally, squeals, "Awww!" and *kisses* that slimy creature smack on the lips! (Eeuew!)

Okay, so you never considered videotaping a child kissing an amphibian as play. But we had fun taping it, unexpected as it was, and it made for a hilarious family memory. Any activity that connects you with your kids in an intimate way, or helps you learn more about your children—and they about you—qualifies as play.

You might think that moment with the salamander just *happened*—that you can't possibly plan such a thing, nor would you necessarily want to! True. But by being open to a potentially funny moment, in the spirit of playfulness, we stopped what we were doing to sprint for the camcorder and pay attention to our daughter. Otherwise we would not have caught "the kiss."

Many times since then, we have watched that tape and laughed together as a family. What a lot of play value for just a few minutes of spontaneous filming!

DOES JUST BEING TOGETHER COUNT AS PLAY?

You may spend a whole day doing kid-related things: chauffeuring children to gymnastics or swimming lessons, doing chores together, even riding in the car on a family vacation. But does any of that qualify as play?

The way you connect during those times may not be conducive to much intimacy and fun. "Hurry, you'll be late for your lesson! What? You can't find your swimsuit? Oh, no, rush-hour traffic is building!" "Yes, you have to clean your room, and I'm tired of nagging you about it." "Hey! Your dad can't drive with you all squabbling in the backseat!" What kind of fun is that?

With a little thought and planning, you *can* use driving time as a way to connect with your kids, although it helps if you're not the one with your eyes on the road.

Does watching children practice, perform, or compete count as play? I'll leave that up to you. That kind of support is extremely meaningful to kids. The image of Mom or Dad in the stands, cheering them on, often creates warm, lasting memories (as parents' absence can create painful ones). But being on the sideline can't entirely replace one-on-one, close contact and conversation. Side-by-side time needs to be balanced with face-to-face time.

COACH, CHEERLEADER, OR SPECTATOR?

What should be our role when we play with our children? As we play, should we tell them what to do, provide words of encouragement, or simply observe, smile, and nod? Is there a "right" way to play with kids—a best way to interact with them?

Arthur Kraft, Ph.D., expert in child psychology, writes about how parents can use creative play to bridge communication gaps with kids.[4] In an informal study, he asked the parents of children he was treating (for anger, anxiety, etc.) to commit to regular, systematic play sessions at home with their children. The parents then met with Kraft weekly, as a group, to describe what had transpired during their play sessions at home with their children. The parents discussed difficult behaviors and puzzling comments that had cropped up in the course of play. They described how they had responded and asked the psychologist what they could have said or done differently.

We can learn valuable techniques from experts to help troubled kids. Kraft's recommended play sessions did effectively improve his little clients' mental health. But I can't help but wonder: Was it because the parents learned to respond to their kids in prescribed ways? Or were the parent-child play sessions successful primarily because the kids were suddenly getting *regularly scheduled, concentrated, one-on-one attention?* There is tremendous power in setting aside focused time to be with our kids. That alone sends them a positive message: *I want to be with you!*

DON'T WORRY ABOUT HOW YOU PLAY

If you have a loving, positive relationship with an emotionally healthy child, please don't worry about using just the right words or actions as you play together. A loving gaze, a warm smile, and attentiveness to your child will make up for many faux pas.

Oops, so you grabbed the scissors too soon, thinking that would help your child. Or you made a suggestion he interpreted as criticism. Suddenly he's having a meltdown. Stuff happens. As long as you avoid hurtful comments and make a genuine effort to show interest in your child, you're likely to find him forgiving of your imperfections.

Do you wonder if it's okay to share your own opinions and feelings about play when you're together? Some believe mutual sharing can be healthy, barring unnecessary criticism or burdening a child with adult troubles. Your child wants to get to know you, as you do him. If your child wants to play an activity in a way that you don't find very interesting, it's perfectly acceptable to say so. You might suggest something you both like, or find a new, fun way to adapt a game he wants to play. (See the tips on pages 147–148 for making Candy Land more fun.)

The more you let your child lead, however, the more you'll learn about the way he thinks. Try not to direct him too much. In fact, there's great freedom in knowing you don't have to make all the decisions. You might be amazed at what a small child will dream up if you just sit or lie still and say, "Let's play!" Don't underestimate your own expertise, knowledge, and understanding of your child. At any given moment, you might be coach, cheerleader, spectator, or a combination of all three! As you can see, there is no particular "right" way to play.

But there *are* common barriers to meaningful playtimes—barriers that cause you to avoid play to begin with or keep you from enjoying play when you do make the effort. In the next chapter, we'll discuss some of the things that get in the way.

5 minute fun

THE UM GAME

This "game" began one day when four-year-old Elisa asked, "Mom, can I have a sandwich with, um, with . . . you know! Um . . ."

"I'm sorry," I replied, very seriously. "We're fresh out of um today!"

"Oh, Mom!" (giggle) "I want some, um . . ."

"We could get some um tomorrow. But it's rather expensive . . ." (Giggle) "Mommy!"

After establishing that it was peanut butter she wanted, and once she was eating, Elisa said, "Now *you* say um, Mom!"

"Okay. I sure would like to . . . um . . ."

"Sorry, Mom, you did that yesterday!" (giggle)

And so the Um Game was born.

An Overview of Barriers

*What? Your playtimes with your children don't
always work out as planned? Ah, yes. Fights erupt.
Yawns take over. Take heart: We all struggle
with at least some barriers to enjoyable
playtimes with our children.*

One afternoon, I sat down to play Memory with three-year-old Aimee and seven-year-old Tyler. Five minutes later, our fun family playtime had degenerated into an hour's worth of tears and tantrums. (That wasn't just the kids.)

You may recall that to play this game, all cards are laid face down. Players take turns flipping two at a time to find matching pairs. Cards that don't match are turned down again; those that do are kept by the player.

Tyler and I had collected piles of cards. Aimee, predictably, due to her age and inexperience, had zero. Of course, big brother could see that poor little sis needed help . . . couldn't he? Hence, when a matching pair became obvious, on my turn I didn't pick it up. Then during Aimee's turn, I hinted to her, "The matching card is in this area," leading her to pick up the set.

"Hey!" Tyler cried out, enraged. "That's cheating!"

"Aw, c'mon Tyler," I replied. "Aimee is still learning how to play. I'm just trying to teach her—the way I taught you, remember?" He didn't remember.

"Look," I tried coaxing pleasantly, "you're winning anyway."

Tyler angrily scattered the cards all over the floor. "You always favor her! You're a cheater!" He was sent to his room for comments that followed.

I handled the whole thing very poorly, trying to defend myself ("No, I'm not cheating. No, I don't favor Aimee over you. . . .") as he kicked and screamed from inside his closed door.

It took a great deal of thought later to figure out why Tyler had reacted as he had, and it took some creative thinking to prevent future mishaps. The kids' individual personalities, age difference, and sibling rivalry had each played a part in our Memory game mess. Since then, I've discovered that understanding differences is a real key to planning successful family activities.

Not that it doesn't take effort, at least initially. Wouldn't it be great if game directions at least hinted at potential land mines we might encounter during play?

I'd love to see these directions added to the Memory game:

> *Warning: If playing this game with two differently aged children, the younger of whom is easygoing yet easily distracted, the older of whom is highly competitive, organized, and goal oriented, do not—I repeat—do not assist the former without the consent of the latter, at the risk of your own mental health.*

What gets in the way of play is often quite complex. Yet it *can* be sorted out and dealt with. And making that effort is worthwhile.

Years ago, one mother I know tried to play a table game with her two boys, but their fighting made it impossible for her to enjoy it. Consequently, she said, "I decided I'd *never* do that again." I remember thinking with some dismay, *How very sad. Never play a game with the kids together again? Truly?*

That conversation stuck in my mind for years, compelling me to write down some of my own struggles with play. It caused me to think more deeply about ways to overcome these struggles and motivated me to not give up too easily. Had I decided after the Memory game incident never to play games with my kids again, I would have missed many delightful opportunities to learn about the ways my children think, to show them how to relate better to each other, and to *enjoy* them. This mother's comment opened my eyes to the fact that not all parents feel the same way about play. Some feel more playful than others.

HOW PLAYFUL DO YOU FEEL?

Many parents enjoy and look forward to playing with their children. A parent who likes to play is likely to integrate a sense of humor into life in general, even activities not necessarily planned as play. However, overscheduling, personality conflicts, health problems, stress, or perfectionism can affect even the most playful parents. Playfulness needs to be balanced with responsibility. We need to find activities that fit us and match our children's developmental needs and limitations. We need validation of our belief that play is valuable.

Or perhaps you feel a general discomfort with play: feeling guilty about taking time for it, feeling uncertain about how to play, or simply lacking joy in it. A parent who feels unplayful may not play with her kids much. She may even think it's unnecessary as long as her child has siblings or friends. Then again, she may play with them often because she feels it is good for them—but she may admit that she doesn't enjoy it very much. Parents like this often struggle especially with spontaneous play.

Allow me to give you an example of what I would call spontaneous play.

One evening, I was making a real effort to get my family to take care of their own clean laundry. After washing and folding it all (whew, almost done!) I took the baskets of clean clothes upstairs for my husband and two children to put away in their dressers. Shortly afterward, I heard hysterical laughter and the booming bass of a stereo.

I found Gordy, Tyler, and Aimee parading around, arms linked, wearing . . . underwear. Just underwear. Underwear as underwear. Underwear as hats. Underwear as masks. Underwear as bracelets. I caught the underwear family on video, dancing on the bed to the hip-hop of D.C. Talk, my husband frantically trying to hide from the camera.

This kind of spontaneous play may sound quite foreign—perhaps even weird—to anyone who did not grow up in a playful household. Your gut reaction might be to wonder, *Did the laundry all get put away?* or *Does she really let them jump on the bed? Is it okay to act that way?*

How do you feel when you read this anecdote about the strange Sargent family? Believe me, we are firm and proper parents when necessary. But we also have an awful lot of fun together.

If you generally feel unplayful, your struggles are primarily internal. Perhaps you feel uncomfortable with play or worry that you haven't enjoyed your children as much as a parent should. Concrete strategies for overcoming external barriers will help you, but your greatest barriers are internal (motivational and emotional). The good news is that both external and internal barriers can be overcome.

PLAY BARRIERS

Barriers to play can be broken into four different categories: time and energy limits, uncertainty about behavior or activities, lack of motivation, and family stress. In part 2, we'll dig more deeply into these barriers. We'll also discuss solutions (with heavy doses of compassion) for dealing with them. But for now, let's just look at an overview of barriers to play.

Which barriers get in your way at the present time? Which ones have presented real struggles for you in the past? Mark any that apply to you.

Barrier #1: Time and Energy Limits
- Hectic work schedules and demands
- Caring for your home and your family's basic needs

- High-need children
- A new baby (feeding, changing, holding)
- Volunteer activities (PTA, church, kids' clubs)
- Illness or injury in extended family
- Child-related activities (sports, music, drama)

Does your busyness interfere in some way with parent-child play and the intimacy it can bring?

Some activities you may choose, such as keeping up with housework, pursuing a career, and volunteering for everything from PTA to Scouts to Sunday school, can crowd out parent-child play. Many of your chosen activities may be child oriented: driving to sports practices and games, or music rehearsals and concerts. You may also rack up mileage driving to and from school.

Other time and energy thieves may press in on you without permission: babies who steal sleep and require countless diaper changes; busy toddlers who need constant diversion from danger; extended family members who are aging, ill, or injured.

Hurried parents often feel guilty about missing out on play but also feel unsure about how to change their situation. Other overly busy parents suspect that parenting should be a more joyful experience but they can't quite see the connection between that feeling and parent-child play, nor how to fit that into their hectic schedules.

If you recognize any of the time and energy barriers listed above, you may be feeling overextended and stressed. You may already grieve having missed a particular stage in your child's life. If so, by prioritizing play more now and finding ways to make your lifestyle less hurried, you can avoid missing future milestones.

No matter how busy you are, you *can* build a more intimate, fun relationship with your child.

Barrier #2: Uncertainty about Activity Choices
- New parenting (how to play with a baby)
- Developmental needs or abilities in one or more children
- Coping with sibling squabbles

⊚ Adapting play for kids with unique learning needs or abilities
⊚ Clashing with strong wills or personality differences
⊚ Choosing appropriate activities and play materials

Are you confused about, or frustrated with, your children's behavior or needs? Are you unsure about what to do with your child, even when you do have the time and energy?

Perhaps you understand your child's behavior—a strong will, high energy level, or low attention span—but aren't sure what to do about it. Do you plan potentially fun activities only to find them falling apart? Do you lack a clear understanding of why things fell apart or what you could have done differently that might have worked better? I certainly felt bewildered when my Memory game turned to disaster.

Perhaps you don't understand your children's personalities or what your kids should be able to do at their current developmental levels. If you try to play but don't enjoy it much, you may not play as often as you and your child need, or you may avoid it altogether. By learning more about what makes you and your children tick, you *can* find ways to play together successfully and more joyfully.

Barrier # 3: Lack of Motivation
⊚ Boredom with child play
⊚ General discomfort with play
⊚ Uncertainty of the value of play
⊚ Seeing playfulness as conflicting with discipline
⊚ Frustration with children's behavior
⊚ Impatience with limited attention spans or messiness
⊚ Awkwardness with spontaneity
⊚ Depression

Are you so well organized and efficient about parenthood that spontaneous play is sometimes difficult for you? Are you less inclined to see yourself as playmate than as caretaker, teacher, and disciplinarian? Perhaps you are unenthused about play or uncomfortable with it—feeling unplayful about life in general.

If you never truly learned how to play, even when you were a child yourself, you may need to learn how. It may take practice to become a little more flexible and more open to playful moments, but there are many very simple ways to play that you can try. The good news is that if you are uncomfortable with play, you are not alone.

Barrier #4: Family Stress
- Colicky baby or seriously ill child
- Crisis pregnancy or difficult pregnancy
- Chronic pain or fatigue
- Marital or financial stress
- General anxiety
- Demands of single parenting
- Stepparenting or adoption of older children
- Substance abuse (in child or adult)
- Chronic illness, injury, or death in extended family
- Serious behavioral problems in a child

Are you temporarily stressed-out—or permanently overwhelmed—by anything in the above list? Why is it that stresses like these are never addressed in books that tell us how to play with our children?

Anxiety, chronic pain, ongoing loss of sleep, or depression can drastically reduce energy or desire for play. A parent who is generally playful may feel guilty and weepy about missing play as a result of family stress. A parent who tends to feel unplayful in general may simply withdraw.

Missing out on playtime with your children may be unavoidable at times. But don't worry. You can make up for those lost play hours once the stress eases. However, it is important to discern whether your stress is long-term (lasting many years) or short-term (weeks or months). Babies with reflux who awaken every two hours not only cause parental sleep deprivation and anxiety over Baby's well-being, but they also may rob parents of time with older children. This may qualify as a temporary stress, although when you are in the midst of it, it seems to last forever.

As for long-term stresses, such as chronic back pain or migraines, play must be gently integrated into life along with other therapies. You don't want those stresses to keep you from experiencing the joys of parenting or cause you to miss entire developmental stages in your children.

Sometimes play, particularly very simple forms of play, can *relieve* stress. It's important to realize that children can be very sensitive to parents' needs and feelings; they can be more flexible and understanding than we often give them credit for. Given the opportunity, they may even comfort us and encourage us to keep our sense of humor. I will show you some touching examples later in the family stress chapter.

But children can also pick up on our stress and become stressed themselves. When this happens, play with you is critical to helping them keep their emotional balance.

Have you been able to identify your own individual play barriers yet? In the upcoming pages, I'll help you analyze your time, prioritize play a little more, and create more time and energy for play. I want you to feel more confident about what to do with your child, no matter what age or personality type he or she is, and find activities that work for your family. I hope you will feel new inspiration and motivation for play even during stressful times.

DON'T SAY IT, SING IT!

When talking to your child, try *singing* your words instead, to a familiar tune. For instance, "Are You Sleeping, Brother John?" ("Frère Jacques") might be sung when you are serving lunch: "Here's your sandwich, here's your sandwich. Eat it now! Eat it now! It is very yummy, delicious in your tummy! Yum yum yum. Yum yum yum."

I've done this for many years, and now Elisa is inventing her own songs, complete with rhyming words.

DRAMATIC FAREWELLS

Surprise your child the next time he says he's going to the bathroom, or just to the other room for a minute. Say, "Send me a postcard!" or "Have a nice trip!" Or you can say with dramatic sobs, "Oh, I'm going to miss you *so* much!"

Benefits of Play

Yes, play can be difficult to plan for or stick with,

but don't give up! It can be so rewarding,

for both you and your child.

our-year-old Elisa was disappointed when her little wooden car didn't win a race at Awana kids' club, where the grand prize had been a trophy. Her brother responded by giving her one of his old basketball trophies. Dad gave her a weight-lifting trophy he'd won at a county fair. Elisa perked up for a while and had fun decorating her room with them.

But later she sighed, "Someday I want to earn a trophy *myself.*"

I asked her, "How would you like to earn one?"

She thought a minute, very seriously. "I think maybe playing soccer . . . or doing gymnastics." She paused. Then she said, matter-of-factly, "But what I really think I want to get one for, someday, is for being a mother, with my own children."

Wow. A mother trophy! Wouldn't that be something?

Just when we as parents feel unappreciated, *BOOM,* a child says or does something to show we are valued. Quite often I've found sweet sentimental messages from Aimee scrolling across the screen saver of my computer. And Tyler enjoys surprising me with breakfast in bed on special occasions, like Mother's Day.

He first did this at about age six or seven. I recall him

waking me and grinning a partially toothless grin from ear to ear as he handed me a breakfast tray. Although I'm rarely hungry the instant I wake up, my child stood expectantly, waiting for me to take that first bite, so I obediently put some scrambled egg in my mouth and chewed. And chewed. And chewed.

In a subtle attempt to uncover the mystery of the rubber eggs, I casually said, "So, tell me how you made this wonderful breakfast!"

Tyler proudly told me how he'd asked Dad to take him to the store so he could use his allowance money to buy me a frozen, premade breakfast. He had set his alarm to get up in the wee hours so he would have enough time to follow all the directions on the package. And I mean *all*. He microwaved the meal, baked it, and I believe he used the toaster oven as well. It was the most inedible and precious breakfast I've ever had in my life.

Although these gifts of appreciation did not occur in the course of play, I do think they are some of the fruits of play. When we play with our children, they recognize it as a gift and eventually find ways to give back. Listed below are five ways you and your child will benefit from playing together. You can use the fingers of your hand as a visual reminder of these ways. Consider the functions or associations with each digit:

Pointer Finger: Teaching/Learning/Curiosity

A toddler points his pudgy dimpled pointer finger at the sky, crying out, "That, that, that!" Mom wonders, *Does he mean, "Look at that"? "What is that?" "Who is that?"* An older child uses his pointer finger to scratch his head as he thinks about what to write in a social-studies report. And have you ever shaken your pointer finger at your child, hoping it would emphasize your point, and said, "I told you, no!" Or do you point it in the air excitedly, saying, "I remember when . . . !"

Learning and teaching through play works both ways. Parent teaches child, and child teaches parent. When Aimee explained to me the difference between "pretend" and "imaginary" cookies, I learned something new about the way my child thought—quite logically, I must say.

But teaching can be a deliberate part of play as well. Through play, you can teach your child some very basic skills, such as hopping, throwing a ball, or holding a pencil. Or you can teach him elaborate games, such as how to play Monopoly—from counting out spaces and money to plotting a winning strategy.

Dr. T. Berry Brazelton, author, pediatrician, and former host of the TV show *What Every Baby Knows,* wrote, "Play is a child's work, and toys are the tools. . . . Different kinds of play can foster different skills, such as language, gross and fine motor movements and imagination."[5] You can teach your child a variety of skills in the course of play. In my former work as a certified occupational therapy assistant, I used play to teach new skills and to observe progress with ongoing skills. Through play, you supplement and build upon the things your child is learning at school.

Play used for teaching is often a more disciplined form of play. But much natural learning can occur through spontaneous play. Alphabet-shaped sponges that stick on the side of the bathtub or your child's body teach him his *ABCs*—under the guise of fun.

Center Finger: Self-Worth/Expressions of Feelings/Comfort

The center finger can represent your child's self-esteem—her sense of being valued and loved simply for who she is. How we feel about ourselves is central to the way we perceive events around us and the way we respond to others. Your interest in your child, regardless of what he does or how well he does it, nurtures this, and it helps him believe that others love him as well, including God. As you play together and offer encouragement, your child's self-confidence grows. That helps him to value others and have compassion for them.

Shari Rusch (Furnstahl), in her book *Stumbling Blocks to Stepping Stones,* describes how, as a small child, everything academic in her life cried out, "Failure!" Shari's mother, however, always believed in her. She taught Shari to cook and restored the feelings of self-worth every child so desperately needs. Despite her severe learning disabilities, Shari's talent for baking earned her a blue ribbon at a county fair.

She was told she'd never get beyond the fifth grade, but Shari eventually achieved—with great difficulty—her master's degree in education. Along with her diplomas, Shari still has that blue ribbon from the fair, a first success stimulated by her mother's encouragement.

Boosting your child's sense of value can have long-lasting effects, building him or her into a more confident adult. As you play, you give your child opportunities to try new things to build his confidence. Even the fact that you set aside time to be with him conveys a strong message: *You are a valuable person.*

Ring Finger: Intimacy

The ring finger represents a heart connection you share with your child. You get to know your child better, as she does you, through one-on-one time you spend together. Your child becomes confident, not just in himself but in the secure relationship he has with you. Through play, you form a bond that's difficult to break, even when stretched to the max during the sometimes-tough teenage years. You build a memory bank of experiences you share, which you can write down or photograph. Later, as you reflect back on those events, you might say, "Remember when we . . . ?" or "You were so funny when you . . . ." This bonds you together further. The time you spend playing becomes an investment in your long-term relationship.

One mother, who was having a tough time with both her marriage and her physical health, told me that in light of those struggles she sees play as a luxury item. She reminded me of Maslow's hierarchy of needs, which reveals how people's basic needs usually have to be met in ascending order.

However, when I looked up that pyramidlike chart, I realized how play helps us meet some of our very basic psychological needs—it truly isn't a luxury item. You see, at the very bottom of the pyramid are the basics: breathing; the need for food, water, and shelter. Next come security and safety needs. Just up from that are needs for love, affection, and a sense of belonging, and those of esteem (self-esteem and the esteem we get from others).

At the tip of the pyramid are needs for self-actualization—realizing your purpose in life and having the desire to help others. That makes sense, doesn't it? It's difficult to feel altruistic or have a sense of purpose if you lack self-confidence and intimacy with others. You have the awesome ability to meet the needs of your child as well as yourself as you play together. The key is in defining parent-child play as *connecting, with a playful attitude* versus *simply engaging in a fun activity.*

A side benefit to achieving more intimacy through play is increased cooperativeness in children. They often follow parents' rules better and decrease their whining and defiance after getting their love tanks filled. When you must say a firm and unequivocal no to your child, he's more likely to believe you truly have his best interests at heart if you have first focused your attention on him in some loving and playful ways. When you promise to play with your child and follow through on that, you show that you are committed to your child, and you reveal your desire to be close to him.

Thumb: Grasp of Broader Concepts

The thumb represents the way we grasp broader concepts and apply them to other situations, just as we use our thumb with opposing fingers to grasp objects. A child practices taking turns playing Memory and gradually learns to take turns kicking a ball on the elementary school playground. He learns from you about the value of specific words of encouragement, and he repeats them to a friend in need. You teach her how to use scissors, and soon she is creating elaborate cards for you and others. You teach him to count as you walk up stairs, and before you know it, he is teaching you algebraic equations.

You also can apply, in a broader way, what *you* learn about your child. Through play, you better understand the way your child thinks and feels, and what his learning style is like. Through play, you see him make progress in areas in which he struggles. You may be the only one offering him praise and encouragement when that progress is not readily apparent to others. This can help you make good educational choices for him—finding the right school or teacher. You will be surprised at how much play teaches you about how someone is thinking, grasping, and changing.

Pinkie: Joy

I suppose we could live without our littlest finger. And yet it makes our hand complete, as joy does with play and parenting in general. I have laughed again and again over funny comments made by a child. One day, tired, I draped myself into a big arm-chair, and four-year-old Elisa flopped down on top of me. I asked her to tell me about some things she'd been doing lately.

She said she'd seen the movie *Pinocchio* at a friend's house, then she burst out, "That mean man put Pinocchio in a cage!"

"He sure was mean. Hmmm. What was his name?" I fought through midlife brain fuzz to recall it, only half-hearing Elisa remark that the man was a big, strong bully.

"He sure was, 'Lisa girl. Oh! I remember—it was Stromboli!"

Elisa replied, impatiently, "That's what I said, Strong Bully."

I have already mentioned that at least one of my children has made me smile nearly every day I've been a parent. Sometimes that joy is a feeling of warm peace rather than outright laughter. Humor can produce joy, but so does our pleasure at seeing our child's new achievements.

When a baby first walks, we often laugh at her funny, awkward, ducklike walk. But we also glow because *that's my baby, and look at her, walking already!* When children achieve new milestones, it's very exciting for their parents. As you increase your awareness of less obvious milestones—for instance, your child's ability to problem solve—you will experience more joy in parent-child play. Joy and laughter are great counterbalances to the stresses in life and the challenges children offer us.

Recent research validates the connection between humor and better health. The American Association for Therapeutic Humor, led by various Ph.D.s, RNs, and other professionals, offers an annual conference and a newsletter, and it aims to "educate health care professionals and lay audiences about the value and therapeutic uses of humor and laughter." As one proverb says, "A glad heart makes a happy face; a broken heart crushes the spirit."[6] Science has shown this proverb to be right on target; optimism is now even being linked to longer life spans.

And so, mixed with the usual parental feelings of exhaustion, frustration, and occasional anxiety, are feelings of expectation, thrill, and the joy of discovery. I'm constantly finding out who these little people are who have been entrusted to me—and what gifts my children truly are. They are a joy to behold when I stop, look, and listen long enough to behold them!

I personally like the image of the hand as a reminder to play, because it's an object that's always with me. When Elisa was only a few hours old, I made a fascinating discovery. Holding her tiny foot in my hand, I realized that it was the exact length of my middle finger. But recently, when I stuck a bandage on a cut on Elisa's foot, I realized that her foot now fills my entire hand.

That same evening I danced with my son—who tried not to step on my toes with his men's size ten shoes—at his ninth-grade graduation. He was startlingly handsome and as tall as me, smiling charmingly, yet blushing with mortification. ("I'll do this, but please don't attract too much attention, Mom.") The dance ended and we unclasped our hands.

I looked at my middle finger. Wasn't his foot just that small not that long ago? Wasn't it only yesterday he giggled as a baby, rolling on the carpet with me? *My, how fast he grew.* Ouch, there's that heart pain again.

minute fun

THREE KISSES

For good-night or anytime, these kisses come in triplets. First, Eskimo Kiss: rub noses with your child. Then, Fishy Kiss: suck in your cheeks and wiggle your lips while smooching. And finally, Butterfly Kiss: take turns batting eyelashes on one another's cheeks!

IMPORTANT APPOINTMENT

If while playing with your child you must answer the phone or door-bell, tell callers or visitors very loudly in front of your child that you have an appointment or a "date" with your child. ("I'm sorry, I have a very important appointment right now and can't be interrupted.")

You can do a planned, organized activity, or you can send your child to get her blocks, a puzzle, or crayons (anything she can create with) and say, "Show me what you can do!" Have her work where you can see her and cheer her on.

chapter 4

Connecting Discipline and Play

How lovely it is when we can spend more time and

energy enjoying our children than controlling them!

Did you know you can balance discipline with

a more playful, loving spirit?

I want to carry that!"

"Okay." I let three-year-old Tyler carry my shopping bag as we walked through the mall with my friend Lynn and her two-year-old daughter.

"Oops, Tyler . . . I don't want that smashed. If you want to carry it, you need to hold the bag by the handle, okay?"

He smashed it, deliberately.

I calmly put it in my purse. Why in the world did he do that?

He walked a few yards away and glared at me.

I ignored it and then tried to distract him. "I'm getting some lemonade. Do you want any?"

No reply.

I figured he'd snap out of his blue funk shortly. But as I finished the purchase and four people took my place in line, he demanded, "*Now* buy *me* one."

"No. I'm not standing in line again. But if you ask more politely, I'll share mine with you."

"No!" he said. "I want my own! I don't want your germs!"

"I'm sorry, it's too late." He scowled and clenched his little fists. I made a quick decision. "Besides, we're leaving the mall right now." I remained calm, yet firm. What a professional mother I was, and here he was, my first child!

"Get me my own lemonade!" *Give it a rest, kid! He usually knows no means no and gives up by now.* But he yelled continuously as we walked the long walk through the mall.

Lynn and I looked at each other. It was definitely time to go.

I tried distracting Tyler again by pointing out a Jeep in a window display. But suddenly, to my absolute astonishment, he began shredding a huge live potted plant in the hallway.

"Tyler, stop that . . . that's someone else's property. I won't let you damage it!" I pulled him away from the plant. He assaulted it again. I was astonished. He'd never acted like that in his life!

I pulled my son into a dressing room in a nearby store, looked him directly in the eyes, and asked what was *really* going on. I knew the issue was not lemonade. But what was it? He tore himself away from me, ran back into the hallway, and attacked the plant again with a vengeance. Lynn and her child stood with mouths agape. Only a few hours before, she had commented on my child's near-perfect behavior at her home. We were visiting Lynn from out of town, and she had baby-sat Tyler the day before.

My voice escalated. "Stop this! Right now! You can walk down this hall by yourself without touching the plants, or I will carry you." You guessed it. He shredded the plant further. I carried forty-pound Tyler kicking and screaming under my arm to the car, worried that if I let go he'd run through the parking lot in a blind rage. Lynn and I fought him further as he braced hands and feet against the car door.

"*Now* I want some of your lemonade!" he screamed.

"Get in the car first. If you're not in by the count of three, I'll dump the lemonade." He refused. I dumped it.

Lynn and I prayed for him to calm down. Remarkably, he settled down enough for us to get him into his car seat in the back. Lynn drove and I sat in the front passenger seat. As we entered heavy traffic, I looked back and saw that Tyler had unbuckled his seat belt. *Aarrgh!* I rebuckled it and held on to his hands. "Tyler, to be safe, you *must* wear your seat belt."

My son, sounding mature and rational, said, "I promise I won't unbuckle it if you let go." I let go. He unbuckled it.

My back hurt from reaching to the backseat. My arms ached from carrying him as he'd thrashed. But I reached back, rebuckled him, and held his hands away from the clasp again. Ouch. How can a little kid take such a physical toll on a grown-up? I tried a new tactic.

"Once there was a boy who worked in a field, protecting sheep."

Tyler relaxed his hands and began listening intently to me.

"As a joke, he yelled, 'Wolf, wolf,' and the townspeople ran to help him. He played that trick three times. The townspeople became very annoyed! Then, when a real wolf came, the boy called out, 'Wolf, wolf!' But nobody came."

Tyler's hands relaxed, and . . . he fell asleep!

Oh, no! Only two minutes later I would have to wake him, then transfer him and his car seat into our own car. I wanted to begin the two-and-a-half-hour drive home before traffic got nasty. Would he go back to sleep, or would he yell and climb out of his seat all the way home?

After waking him with great fear and trepidation, I opted to spend fifteen minutes with him before we left. I cuddled him in an armchair, read him a story, stroked his hair, and told him I loved him. Then, miracle of miracles . . . He was delightful the entire way home; he was the child I'd always known. And an amazing thing happened. Out of the blue, he retold me the cry-wolf story, then said, "Mom, I'm not gonna tell lies."

"That's good, honey." Hmm, where did that come from?

"But I did today."

"You did?"

"When I unbuckled my seat belt after I said I wouldn't. But I'm not gonna lie anymore, like that boy who said wolf."

I was stunned. In the midst of a tantrum he'd heard that message? To think that even when he was out-of-control and emotionally overwrought, his little mind was still working . . . hmmm. I'm convinced that children are much more complex than we give them credit for.

I thought later about how I'd handled Tyler's tantrum. I'd maintained my cool most of the time, offering some consequences and follow-through, but to no avail. Several days later he had a fever and a cough. Could I blame it all on that?

Then it hit me as I considered our trip from his perspective. Two days before, I had strapped Tyler into a car seat for nearly three hours as we drove from our home on the coast to the Seattle area so I could attend a conference. Then I had dumped him unceremoniously at a stranger's house (Lynn was a stranger to *him,* anyway). When I had finally returned from the conference, I gabbed with my friend instead of focusing on my child, despite his efforts to get my attention. We had slept restlessly in that strange house, and in the morning, although he had *begged* me to lay still and cuddle him, I had insisted we go downtown "for fun!" He had sobbed when I buckled him into his car seat in the back. "I want to sit in front, with you!"

We had managed to boost his mood with a trolley ride, so optimistically (too optimistically) Lynn and I had told him we were making a quick trip to the mall. As soon as we got there, I had the nerve to abandon him again, with Lynn. Why? To go fetch a package, the very same package in the shopping bag he crushed, which ultimately began the terrible tantrum, leading to his emotional point of no return.

Twelve years and two children wiser, I still can't think of much I could have done differently to prevent him from shredding that plant—except to skip going to the mall in the first place. But I was absolutely on target about one thing: Lemonade had definitely not been the issue. And in the end, I was amazed that it required only fifteen minutes of focused cuddle time—a little bit of play—to make things all better. And it taught me a great lesson: Discipline and play are intricately woven together. A child's behavior can be *directly* affected by his need to connect with Mom or Dad. I learned that some situations requiring discipline can be eliminated before they ever start by first meeting a child's need for attention.

VERBALIZING THE NEED FOR ATTENTION

Unfortunately, even when we're prepared to respond to a child's request for attention, a preschooler can't always tell us he needs it. It can be difficult for a child that age to connect feelings of frustration and anger with a need to get his or her love tank filled. And even when a child does realize that's what he wants, even when equipped with a normal—or advanced—vocabulary level, the child may not be able to verbalize those feelings. Although Tyler was able to connect the moral of the wolf story with his lying about his seat belt, he was not able to connect his rage about lemonade with his need for focused attention.

You may wonder how I connected the two myself. One clue was that Tyler's behavior was entirely out of character. Before that day (and ever since) he has been a kid who generally follows directions and is a delight to be around. Never before had he raged like that over not getting something he wanted, especially anything so minor as lemonade. That episode was bizarre and baffling enough to make me stop and think: What could the true reason behind his behavior be?

Since then, I've tried to teach my kids to tell me directly when they need attention, instead of whining or acting out. This is especially helpful when I must prepare meals or work on the computer—when I'm available, yet not available. Aimee grasped this concept as early as two and a half years old. One day she tugged on my shirt as I washed the dishes.

"Want some 'tension?" she asked.

No thanks, I have enough tension! . . . Oh, I get it. . . .

"Sure, I'll give you some attention. I just need ten minutes to finish here. Let me set the timer, okay?" (I thought it interesting that the way she phrased it held a hidden truth: Adults need attention and forget to ask for it too!) Knowing that a quick cuddle was forthcoming helped her to occupy herself for those ten minutes.

However, some personalities have more difficulty expressing their needs with words. From the time she could toddle, Elisa has always been more inclined to throw darts from her dark eyes and run to her room when angry than to verbalize her feelings. When she was young we had to begin working on this in earnest, telling her outright when she needed to use words to help us know how she felt. One incident brought this to the forefront.

I SHOULD HAVE SEEN THE WRITING ON THE WALL

I had been working feverishly to meet a deadline for a magazine article. Then I noticed that Elisa, nearly four years old, was awfully quiet . . . too quiet. I began searching the house for her and came upon a wet towel lying in the middle of the hall, smeared with red and blue marker.

Then I found some scribbles on the wall, which the towel had apparently not rubbed off, along with Elisa's trademark signature with a backwards *L*.

" 'Lisa . . . where are you?" I called out.

"Under the bed," I heard a voice say quietly from her room.

I went to her room. "Why are you under your bed?"

I heard the hidden voice reply, hesitantly, "Because . . . I'm not the one who drew on the wall."

Of course her guilt was obvious. She had signed her work. She had to clean up her mess, although she had already tried, knowing I would expect that. The wall did not come clean easily, but thanks to the markers being washable, it did at last.

The conversation that followed was most intriguing. I finally got it out of her that she was upset that I'd been ignoring her. I asked her if she thought that drawing on the wall (and having to scrub it clean) was a good way to express that anger. And this amazingly introspective little person said, "No. And hitting people or calling them names or breaking things is not a good way either."

There was a funny side to this incident. Ironically, the article that I had been working on at that very moment had been on, believe it or not, how to teach small children to use art materials appropriately. Gee, how I hate those little lessons in humility!

DERAILING DISRUPTIVE BEHAVIOR

We've talked about how a child's desire for attention can cause him to act out. However, it does take some practice as parents to discern whether or not difficult behavior is simply a ploy to get Mom or Dad to play. If the only time you play with a child is after he has acted out (or whined excessively), the child is likely to see playtime as a reward for unpleasant behavior. You don't want that, of course—but neither should time with you be seen as a reward for good behavior. Your child needs to know that your decision to play with him is made simply because you love him, unconditionally, and that you want to be with him.

But what if a child is so difficult that your desire for play—or to be with him at all—is zapped? The general level of cooperation between you and your child will certainly affect your own feelings of playfulness. Also, you may find you have little time and energy left for play if you're spending it dealing with defiant, disagreeable, or out-of-control behavior.

Your child's level of cooperation is affected not only by how his emotional needs are being met but also by:

- Realistic expectations for a child his age
- Clear and fair rules
- Clear consequences, consistency in enforcing them, and your attitude when enforcing them

REALISTIC EXPECTATIONS

If your expectations for your child are in line with her or his developmental needs and abilities, you will be less likely to set yourself and your child up for failure. For example, it's unwise to set five colors of Play-Doh on a coffee table in the living room—over your nice carpet—at a three-year-old's birthday party. In a child's eagerness to use everything he sees (not to mention being distracted by other things going on in the room), material is certain to end up smashed underfoot, and the rainbow of colors may quickly turn into a muddy ball. Even when he's only playing with you, if you offer your small child too much choice, he is likely to feel overwhelmed. He is uncertain about what to do with it all, then gets frustrated and rebellious about having to clean it up. You might spend half the play date telling him what to clean up. Keep in mind that small children are often very content to play with a single color and a choice of tools to use with it.

Realistic expectations take into consideration a child's individual personality as well as his developmental level.

CLEAR AND FAIR RULES

Clear and fair rules are not easy to come by. One of the most difficult aspects of parenthood is deciding when to say no—or yes—to behavior or requests. We don't always have time or energy to think before making decisions. Decisions about your child's behavior or requests are usually based on one of four criteria:

- ☉ You want to keep your child safe
- ☉ You want her to become more independent and learn to care for herself
- ☉ You want to instill a particular value in her (responsibility, kindness, respect for others)
- ☉ You want to avoid inconvenience for yourself

Any one of the reasons above may cause you to tell your child what he should (or should not) do, although if you frequently say no simply because the request inconveniences you, it may build resentment in him. You might ask yourself, *Is what he wants to do really* that *dangerous? or destructive? or inconvenient?* Will your decision truly help instill the value you hope for, or is your child old enough to learn from his own consequences? If problem behavior occurs in the midst of playing with you, can you gently guide your child in another direction to keep the positive momentum going?

Constantly citing new rules to children is time consuming.

Wouldn't you rather spend that time playing together? One big help is to establish firm, broad rules. This works even with older babies and young toddlers. Once you have made it clear to your diapered explorer that touching the light socket or pulling ribbons out of videotapes is a no-no, try the following: Get down to your child's level, look him straight in the eye, and say quite firmly, "You obey Mama" (or Papa).

I'm not talking about mere curious exploration. I'm referring to those moments when your little cutie crawls over to do something you just told him not to do ("Don't touch that socket, it can hurt you") but first stops and grins at you. He *knows* he's disobeying but finds the attention it garners rather fun. Hearing "You obey Mama" repeatedly gets rather boring and takes some fun out of it all and will help you to be more consistent, because you won't have to creatively explain every single no.

On a walk with a toddler, instead of saying, "No, don't pull up that plant," and "No, don't step on those flowers," and "You can't take the ball out of that yard" (three rules), you lump them together into one: "We don't disturb other people's property without their permission." One rule.

You can also weave the importance of honoring others into casual conversations with a child, as you play or walk in the neighborhood together. Aimee was only about three when I overheard her tell another child, "That person must have worked really hard to make their garden pretty, so we don't pick their flowers." Understanding general moral reasons behind rules can help children regulate *themselves* instead of our having to control them incessantly.

With an especially strong-willed or energetic child, you may need to be more creative about making rules into choices. Almost any "choice" will do (this helps a child feel a little in control), but be sure you can live with any choice you offer. Incorporating play into expectations often helps as well. For example, toothbrush games. The child must brush his teeth but can choose the game. (See Five-Minute Fun on page 146.)

You can also incorporate choices into play itself. This is an especially good way to handle misbehavior during playtimes. One day when Elisa was playing with her friend Alexandra, they were arguing, pulling a toy back and forth. Instead of declaring a rule: "No fighting. Share your toys," I said, "Guess what, girls? You have a choice here. You can either do this . . . " (I exaggerated pulling the toy back and forth, crying loudly, "No! Mine! Mine!") "for the rest of your play date, which is only for a half-hour more, or you can choose to do something else. It's up to you. What do you think sounds like the most fun?" They looked startled, giggled at my antics, then ran off together debating how best to spend the time left.

Even children who follow directions well after rules are set may challenge rules as they are being decided upon. Some kids seem to be little defense lawyers, compelled to seek logical reasons for rules and consequences and often coming up with logical alternatives and compromises. But often you must say no, period, discussion ended, when you know the child's limited experience and understanding won't make your reasoning logical to him anyway. Sometimes a gut feeling, a general uneasiness, may prompt you to say, "I know you can't understand why I'm saying no. But I guarantee that it's because I love you."

Will your child believe that? Most likely, if you've demonstrated your love with undivided attention and affection, especially in parent-child play. If, during more playful moments, your child sees you as a fair and loving person (less bent on controlling than on guiding and nurturing), he'll be more likely to accept your rules.

CLEAR AND CONSISTENT CONSEQUENCES

The best consequences can be difficult to decide upon and enforce. It usually helps if your child knows the consequences before he misbehaves and if they are directly connected to the infraction. For instance, when Elisa drew on the wall, she *knew* that a consequence would be having to clean up her mess—the wet towel revealed her understanding of that.

Of course, kids often do things we can't anticipate, at which time we must put our thinking caps on. Once when six-year-old Tyler got too rough and wild with his baby-sitter and she swore she'd never watch him again, Tyler had to choose between going to bed early for a week or weeding the front yard. Although those consequences were not directly related to sitter abuse, we knew he hated both consequences and we needed to make a strong impression. He chose the yard and became a baby-sitter's dream child thereafter. And a surprise to us was how proud he was about the job he did weeding!

Enforcing consequences often requires tremendous creativity and energy. It can be inconvenient and time consuming! However, if your children repeatedly ignore your requests—and you do nothing about it—it's not likely in light of your frustration that you will want to play with them.

It's not nearly as fun to enforce discipline as it is to play! Yet when discipline is administered sensitively and promptly, your child will see both play *and* discipline as demonstrations of your love. You are also likely to find that the more consistent you are, the less time and energy you spend in the long run having to control your children. And your children are more likely to see that consequences occur as a direct result of their *choices*.

For help in developing realistic consequences, I recommend the book *Choices Are Not Child's Play: Helping Your Kids Make Wise Decisions,* by Pat Holt and Grace Ketterman, M.D. The authors show how far-reaching your consistency can be: "For every choice in life, there is a consequence. The child assumes responsibility for his choices, and learns how to make wise decisions and prevent future mistakes. The child is given more options and greater opportunities to make increasingly complex choices."[7]

You don't have to be your child's buddy all the time to retain a playful relationship. You *can* be firm, yet fun!

Of course, there will be days when your child's behavior or emotions are out of control. No matter how consistent you are, nothing seems to help. There may be an overriding physical need (hunger, exhaustion, or illness) leading to disruptive behavior, especially with small children. But if your child is continuously out of control and you struggle with constant feelings of frustration because of it, seek out some good resources and support from others to help you learn how to apply logical consequences to misbehavior.

Which comes first: the chicken or the egg? discipline or play? When you are clear, consistent, fair, and loving, your child will be more cooperative. When he is more cooperative, you're likely to feel more playful. When you play, your child feels loved and will be less likely to seek negative attention. Which comes first? It's hard to tell. Discipline and play are intertwined.

IT AIN'T EASY

Being a firm and consistent disciplinarian is never as easy as experts tend to make it seem. The level of discipline in my own home has been influenced at various times by my children's ages and temperaments, my health, and my workload. With PMS and a 1040 tax form due in the mail the next day, I'm not at my best. When under stress, you may find yourself saying yes to things you'd normally say no to and then regret it later. Or you might say no too sharply, provoking hurt feelings and outbursts of negative behavior by your children.

We should not make excuses when we goof in the discipline department. I've asked my kids' forgiveness at times when I've been either too strict or too lenient. It helps to reflect periodically on what works and what doesn't, recommitting yourself to consistency.

At the same time, we need to give other parents a bit more grace and less judgment. The next time you see a child in a mall tearing apart foliage, consider that his parent may be as startled as you. Her parenting skills are being put to a sudden—and rather unfair—test before an audience. And the cause of her child's behavior may be a real mystery, as is the solution!

Perhaps the parent is an inconsistent disciplinarian . . . perhaps not. Mall meltdowns are often caused by simple hunger or exhaustion in little ones who can't cope well emotionally with those physical symptoms. Then again, the cause may be deeper than that, deep down to the simple need for some dedicated, one-on-one Mommy or Daddy time.

5 minute fun

FOILED

Grab anything that can be twisted to look remotely like a bow—a bread-bag twisty, a hair doodad, some bow-tie macaroni—and hold it under your nose, as if it were a mustache.

In a nasal voice, sneer, "You must pay the rent!"

Move the bow to the top of your head and in a high voice insist, "But I *can't* pay the rent!"

Repeat this a few times. Then hold the bow under your chin, like a bow tie, and in a more gallant voice, say, "*I'll* pay the rent!"

Back to the hair bow: "Oh, my hero!"

Then to the mustache again: "Curses! Foiled again!"

INTERRUPTION FUN

Once your children know that interrupting you while you visit with friends is usually a no-no and they are very good at being polite, you might surprise them on occasion. When your child and your friend's child are playing near enough to overhear you, look your friend straight in the eye and talk as if you are continuing a real adult conversation.

Say, "You know, I really need to . . ." then leap at the children, screeching, "*tickle* some children!" As they run giggling away, you go back to your real conversation, until you see them sneak back eagerly for round two. Draw your next line (it can be anything) out a little longer to build suspense (look very seriously at your friend, not at the children): "Do you remember last week when I decided it was very, very important to . . . *tickle those kids!!*"

BE AN ACTOR

Ask your child to show you, with his face and body, the following emotions: sad, happy, angry, proud, frustrated, etc. Have him act out a scene that might make him feel that way. Have your child pantomime being an animal for you to guess, or even something like toast popping out of a toaster.

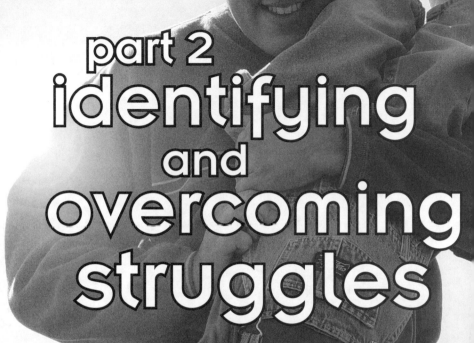

part 2
identifying
and
overcoming
struggles

chapter 5

Time and Energy Barriers

Is your busy schedule preventing you from spending

precious moments with your children? Your busyness

may even be child-related, if you find, as Wilma

Flintstone did, "Between Pebbles, the dishes, and the

wash, nothing is ever dry at the same time." Let's

find some ways to make time for play—to enjoy our

kids when they are small!

Six-year-old Tyler usually burst in the door after walking the block home from school every day. Some days he proudly said, "Look at my math paper!" or waved a dinosaur diorama for me to *ooh* and *aah* over. Other days, he dragged in, downcast. He needed a hug and a neon green Band-Aid after a fall from the monkey bars. Once he came in quietly, sporting a gorgeous smile with gaps from missing teeth, and whispered to me about his "girlfriend," revealing a stick-figure drawing of them smooching. (I could smile but didn't dare laugh.)

I *usually* tried to be available to him after school, as it tended to be a good moment for us to connect. But I was to learn the hard way how meaningful that was to my son.

One day, my eyes were magnetized to the computer screen, my hands to the keyboard. I'd been frantically working for hours to meet a deadline. Suddenly the slamming of the front door, down the hall, startled me. With shock and disbelief, I checked my watch. Three o'clock *already?*

Oh, no! I slapped my hand to my forehead. I had planned

to pick up Aimee, then a toddler, at 2:30 at the sitter's house, then rush back in time to beat Tyler home. I could have kicked myself for not watching the time!

I flew out of the office, tossing papers in my knee-deep TO FILE pile as I went.

"Hey, Tyler! We've got to run and get your sister." No answer. Where could that kid be?

I heard footsteps thump-thump up the stairs and called again impatiently, "Come on, honey . . . I've got to get going."

Assuming he'd heard me, I hunted for car keys and shoes. Several minutes later, jacket in hand, I called again. "Tyler, let's go!" I was getting annoyed.

Slam! There went the front door again. What? I thought he was upstairs! But through our front window, I glimpsed his small figure hiding behind a bush. I had no time for games. I lost what was left of my cool, stomped to the door and opened it, then yelled, "Tyler, you get in here *right now!* I'm late picking up Aimee!"

INDEPENDENT PLAY

Some preschoolers play happily by themselves, while others hate to be alone. You may find that occasionally, you need some time to recharge in order to be a less stressed parent and a better friend to your child.

To help nurture independent play in your child, try the following:

Fill Your Child's Tank
When your child's emotional tank is low (often indicated by whining) she needs to be filled with focused conversation and attention before feeling secure enough to keep going on her own. To fill her tank:

Set aside a specific time for play with your child. This way, he'll be more likely to wait patiently.

Pinpoint your child's needy times. Is your extrovert an early riser? Plan tonight for an activity to do together early tomorrow. Perhaps your child is needy immediately after preschool. Spend a few minutes before she gets home to wind down and get "psyched up" to be with her.

Try activities together that your child can continue alone, and keep materials available. After you teach a child to fold construction paper and color it to make cards, he might binge on card making. Remember, paper is cheap.

Take time to arrange play dates for her with other children. If these happen at your home, consider playing wholeheartedly with them. If you need to get chores done, invite over kids who can play independently and responsibly with your child.

Tyler flew into the house at my request.

But to my astonishment, he stormed past me to the stairs inside. He threw himself onto the bottom step. He crumpled into a ball, sobbing, his little fists pressed against his eyes.

I was flabbergasted. "What's the matter, Honey?"

Tyler suddenly sat upright and cried out, with tears running down his face, "Don't you know it's *May Day?*" He buried his face in his hands.

I was baffled. "What do you mean?"

Tears streamed down his dusty face as he wailed, "How come you didn't pick it up? You opened the door, and you didn't even pick it up!" He leaned against the wall where he sat and sobbed as if his heart would break.

Confused, I went to the front porch. There lay a droopy dandelion on the mud-caked doormat—minus a few petals, but an accusing yellow beacon nonetheless. As I picked up his surprise present, guilt crashed down on me. My excuses dribbled out weakly: about

---

Top off the Tank Periodically

A true extrovert needs more than one fill-up per day. Experts say parents should expect their extroverted children to spend only small chunks of time alone. To keep your socialite satisfied yet still get work done:

Involve her in household tasks as your sanity allows. It may lengthen the task and shorten your patience, but remind yourself that your child enjoys the time with you and can learn from chores as well. Try talking your way through activities: "Now, let's find the eggs for breakfast."

Use small bits of time (five to ten minutes), while in the car or doing dishes, to play word games, like those in the Five-Minute Fun sections. This will help satisfy your child's need to talk and play with language.

Idle Time

After doing the above, let your child know when you both need a break.

One day after devoting time to my daughter, I said, "We've had Aimee time, now it's Mommy time." I explained that I needed quiet time. To my astonishment, she complied by looking at books on her own. Your child may respond to this best if it's part of a predictable schedule. Say, "After lunch, we both need quiet time." Help her gather her own supply of quiet toys, picture books, or art materials. (Limit videos if you want your child to learn to play alone.) Express appreciation to your child for giving you time, and praise her for being independent.

deadlines, and stress, and promises to the sitter, and the fact that it was still April, not yet May, and I'd never been given a May flower, and . . .

Then I realized how stupid my reasoning must sound to a small child who had planned a surprise of such magnitude. His flower had gone unnoticed, his act of love unappreciated. And he'd gotten yelled at, to boot.

I told Tyler how sorry I was and tried taking him in my arms. Angrily, he pushed me away and continued to cry. I asked him to forgive me, thanked him for his thoughtfulness, and told him how much I loved him. Gradually his slender back stopped shaking and his cries dwindled to sniffles. He allowed me to hug him briefly as he fiddled with the untied laces on his G.I. Joe sneakers. Finally he stood, and as I pulled him towards me, he buried his face in my shirt. I stroked his hair, and he leaned into me limply.

With great ceremony, I placed his dandelion into an empty 7-UP bottle with a little water. I set it on the windowsill, and sunlight glistened through the green container with its yellow-petaled crown. I offered to buy Tyler a treat on the way to the baby-sitter, to show my appreciation in a tangible way. We were late to the sitter anyway; I just hoped she would feel sympathy when she heard the reason for my tardiness.

Still looking a bit depressed, Tyler agonized at the Quick Stop between a 50-cent Popsicle and a $1.60 fancy ice cream bar. Guess which one he picked. (Oh, well; I had at least $1.60 worth of guilt to spend.) He told me how good it tasted. As we began to chat about his day, the tension dissipated out the open car windows. Within a half-mile he offered me a bite, and I knew that we were okay with each other again—although I also knew that at 3:05 the next day, I had an appointment to keep with my son.

Even now, when I hear the distress cry "May Day! May Day!" in military movies, I'm reminded of that moment when my distraction and busyness created real distress for my child. I nearly missed receiving a lovingly chosen gift. I find it significant that before that particular day, I had often used that after-school time to show my love for him—but on that day, he chose it to show his love for me.

All parents are busy, but there are times when that busyness is more extreme. Right now, you might be experiencing extremely limited time and energy and you may wonder how in the world you'll ever find time for play. Start by taking a good look at the types of activities that fill your days. Break your activities into three categories:

- Activities you *must* do and have little control over
- Activities you must do, yet have *some* control over (you can schedule, delegate, or simplify them)
- Activities you *choose*—some eagerly and with forethought, some without either

Working until my son came home from school was an activity I *chose*. I also chose to connect with Tyler at that time of day when he was that age, because it fit our schedules and his particular needs. As Tyler reached his preteen years, he preferred long talks before bed. Now that's he's a teen, I miss those days. I wish I'd chosen to take advantage of that more often, instead of being in such a hurry to get the kids to sleep so I could go to bed myself or have some quiet, kid-free time. Now that Tyler doesn't ask to be tucked in at night anymore, I sometimes wish he would.

You may find other times when you and your children best connect. I urge you to plan for those times, lest you miss a tender moment when your child suddenly bounces back to you the affection you have tossed his way over and over again.

First, let's explore those activities you have little control over. Consider the next few pages of this chapter to be a compassionate hug from me to you. It's a hug for those days when absolutely nothing on your to-do list gets finished—those days when you crawl into bed late at night wondering what in the world you did all day and why it made you *so* exhausted. Those of you with little ones will identify most, but all of us remember days like that.

ACTIVITIES YOU MUST DO (BUT CAN'T EASILY CONTROL)

Some activities we know about in advance accompany major choices. But that doesn't make doing them any easier. For instance, you knew that having a baby would mean doing diaper duty. But I'll bet you didn't know it would take twelve to fourteen hours a week and require 2,190 diaper changes within a year! What about sleep? Knowing ahead of time that new babies wake during the night does not mean you can predict when or how often your own baby will wake, nor how long she will want to party in the moonlight.

This loss of control is especially difficult for parents with first babies, or those who previously organized their time well, perhaps in the workplace. For parents of small children, even the most perfectly planned day may go awry.

Plan in Pencil, Not Ink

Picture a mother heading out the door with a fed, diapered, sweet-smelling infant, just in time to get Big Sis to a swimming lesson. As Mom buckles in Baby, she finds him suddenly not so sweet smelling. She unbuckles and picks up the leaky child, holds him close, then discovers she too now needs a change of clothes. Back they all go into the house, to get ready again . . . during which time Sister loses her shoes. Unless Mom has built an extra half hour into her schedule, that swimming lesson may have to be crossed off the calendar.

There are segments along the parenting time line when a few hours become wonderfully predictable. A baby finally sleeps through the night. A toddler naps like clockwork—every day, for two hours after lunch. Then *boom!* Just when you've established a routine, your busy-bee toddler outgrows naps. Then she becomes a preschooler who wakes you at night because there's a dragon in her room, or her tummy feels urpy. Everyone knows mommies and daddies make things all better. (If only it were always true.)

Even when children become teens, the unexpected can happen. One day I got a call from my son's junior high because Tyler had stapled his finger. The school nurse said since it was an impaled object—*impaled object?* ugh!—a parent had to come to the school to remove it. As your own children grow older (and start driving!) you may find that your loss of some control becomes less frustrating, yet more worrisome.

Compounding the inability to plan your time may be the number of children you have, how closely spaced in age they are, and their personalities and individual abilities. Some children are naturally more dependent and need more attention or supervision. Some with disabilities need more help with basic needs.

No matter what, one key word closely associated with child rearing is *unpredictability*. At least parenting is no boring assembly-line job. And yet the excitement of unpredictability often blends with the mundane. Daily chores must be done daily—and often go unnoticed unless *not* finished. And with small children around, finishing anything can be difficult—the dishes, a sentence, even a thought!

Many chores must be redone shortly after you are proud to have completed them. Shortly after you've mopped the floor, the contents of a glass of sticky orange juice are splashed across the kitchen. Some days may seem like a comedy of errors, and you may find yourself repeatedly sighing or perhaps engaging in some maniacal laughter.

Illnesses or injuries to yourself, your spouse, or an extended family member are another unpredictable time stealer. When my mother had a stroke, I flew down to California with twenty-two-month-old Aimee. The ensuing weeks revolved around the care of my mother as well as my child, plus juggling Tyler's schedule with Gordy from afar.

Years later, Tyler enthusiastically leapt on me for a hug/wrestle. I inadvertently caught my ankle under the couch. I spent the next month using my crutches to herd baby Elisa down the hall to her changing table. A difficult pregnancy can incapacitate a mother as well. Bed rest must be excruciating for anyone who loves to be on the move. But while this robs you of energy and movement, you may end up with a gift of time with older children, when all you can do is lie still and watch or cuddle them.

In addition to accepting the unpredictable nature of parenting, I also suggest that you:

Accept Your Limitations and Note Your Accomplishments

On days when nothing seems predictable and it seems that you are getting nothing done that you actually planned to do, have mercy on yourself. Remember that what you're doing as a parent, nurturing the growth of another human being—perhaps more than one—is extremely valuable.

Tammy, mother of a two-year-old and a ten-month-old, e-mailed me: "At this very moment, I am trying to type this with Ebby on my lap nursing. Brandon is behind my chair, brushing my hair while I tell him to stop, be careful, not being as patient as I should be."

Tammy writes, "I feel embarrassed when people come over at 2 P.M. and we are not yet dressed, and the house is trashed." But, she continues, "It helps when I'm not putting pressure on myself to keep the house spic-and-span. My husband doesn't criticize, which is wonderful." She sees nursing and playing with her children as valuable and rewarding. In fact, she is more likely to feel guilty when her son watches a movie instead of playing with her than when there are crushed crackers in the carpet. She knows the time to play with her children while they are so young is fleeting.

Tammy says she believes her job as a mother is ordained—that her children were chosen just for her. That gives her a sense of purpose even when parenting is difficult. "God gave me a wild, strong-willed, active boy," she writes, "then a mellow, sweet girl because I'd have gone crazy with two out-of-control children! He knows what we can take, and what type of children will help mold our characters."

At the end of a long, seemingly fruitless day, write down everything you did, including comforting, playing with, or teaching your child. Perhaps your child has helped mold *your* character! Did you learn, today, how to be a little more patient? a bit more creative?

If you fall into bed exhausted before you can recall what you accomplished that day, at least remain hopeful. There's always tomorrow.

Seek Support

Parenting groups are a great way to lift your spirits if you're at a stage of parenthood when your schedule is largely out of your control. That may seem rather illogical—after all, it takes some planning to get to a meeting in the first place! On days when you feel overwhelmed, you may actually feel guilty about going to a play group. But that's probably when you most need it. It's really helpful to hear other parents confess they don't have everything under control, including their time.

Many support groups offer activities for both you and your children. Those activities include group field trips and craft projects to presentations by parenting experts. But often the most important ingredient is commiseration with other parents who know what you're going through and how you feel. For more information on finding a good support group, see the sidebar on pages 186–187.

Keep Your Sense of Humor

My Aimee has adored shoes from the time she was a toddler. One day when she was about two, I was trying to get out the door to go to the grocery store. I thought Aimee was ready, but to my exasperation I found her in her room, surrounded by every sock and shoe she owned.

She had managed to put on both black dress shoes, but she had a red knee sock on one foot and a white lacy anklet sock on the other. I was in a hurry and not up for a battle, so I decided to take her to the store just like that.

Aimee was delighted, yet no doubt surprised, by the many smiles, nods, and winks from strangers in the checkout line who said, "Ooh, what a big girl you are!" or other such things. They were responding to the sign I had written and taped onto Aimee's back before we left home that said: I DRESSED MYSELF!

Be open to the funny stuff, and take advantage of it sometimes. It may bring a bit of laughter to others besides yourself.

When your child says something funny, write it down and tell it to others. Give that funny moment more mileage. You might even get cash for it, as I did this one, printed in a magazine and later in a flip calendar:

> *While driving with my two-year-old to the sitter one day, I heard him announce from the backseat, "Mom, I have to go pee!"*
>
> *Since this was his first car trip diaperless (in his brand new Mickey Mouse underwear), there was a definite urgency to the situation. Calmly I replied, "Well, honey, we're almost there. You'll just have to hold it."*
>
> *I looked in my rearview mirror to see him groping frantically at his booster seat (which had a bar across the front). With panic on his face, he cried out, "But I can't reach it!"*[8]

Keep the Big Picture in Mind

Your child is rapidly growing. I know it's hard to remember or even believe this if you're facing seemingly never-ending days of diapers or potty trips. Look for developmental milestones your child reaches along the way. This will make parenting more fun for you and it will make the time pass faster as well—too fast, believe it or not. When it seems that nothing else gets done in a day, time you spend with your child is precious.

ACTIVITIES YOU CAN CONTROL—A LITTLE

Next on your to-do list are activities you must do yet can plan to some extent. Your family must eat. Your kids need to have clean clothes, go to the dentist, and get to school on time. You also have to pay bills, do some tax preparation, and get your house clean somehow. If you are a single parent or if finances are tight, it's likely that you must work outside of the home.

How can you control activities like this? I suggest *simplifying, delegating,* or *clustering.* For instance, you can simplify by getting a premade pizza instead of making a meal from scratch. You can delegate laundry and housecleaning duties to your kids and your spouse—perhaps you can even splurge and hire someone. (I wish! Sigh.) You can cluster appointments and shopping trips as much as possible. It may not always work out that way, but usually you will have some options if you think creatively.

If you're working to help provide income for the family, it's possible you may have some control over your hours or the type of job you take. Can you work part-time from home or scale down your living expenses to enjoy more time with your kids while they are small?

In the great working parent versus stay-at-home parent debate, I plant my feet in both camps, working part-time with an office in the home. Whether you work inside the home or away, it takes some very creative thinking and much delegating of household tasks to squeeze in family time. But you can do it. Here are a few ideas:

Do Tasks at Unconventional Times

Even if you do want to do things yourself, you may be able to alter when you do them and involve your children somehow. If, like me, you feel spent by 5:00 P.M., consider making lasagna in the morning, with your child doing the layering. To you, it's dinner; to him, it's an art project!

You can also whip together and freeze a whole batch of meals on a Saturday by using a once-a-month cookbook or your favorite freezer recipes. For that type of cooking, you create bowls full of prepared ingredients, say five cups of grated cheese, a bowl of chopped onion, etc., then throw meals together assembly-line fashion. I've cooked up an unbelievable sixteen dinners in one day with the kids helping (and they even learned some math skills while measuring).

The best thing about this routine is that in the following weeks there are no pots and pans to wash—only plates. And at 5:00 P.M. when you are tired, instead of scrambling to figure out what to fix for dinner, you can throw a meal from freezer to oven and cuddle your child in the recliner while you read him a story.

Nurture Children's Self-Reliance

You'll be amazed at how quickly your child can learn to do things by himself. Even a four-year-old can whip up his own peanut butter sandwich, although he may still want you to cut the crusts off! Your child's self-reliance will not only help you save time, it will make your child feel good about himself or herself.

I saw evidence of this at a most unlikely time, when one evening, Elisa was experiencing excruciating pain from a blistered eardrum. Despite the fact that I had used pain medication, ear drops, and a hot pad, my normally stoic child had cried for hours. I rubbed her back and sang to her. Included in my repertoire, following "I've Been Workin' on the Railroad" and "You Are My Sunshine," was "Jesus Loves Me," including the line "We are weak, but he is strong." Elisa bolted upright despite her pain, with tears still on her face, and said, "Yeah, but some children are strong. I can carry a gallon of milk in and out of the fridge." She certainly does, and pours it too, after getting her own cereal, bowl, and spoon.

Inject Play into the Mundane

In the movie *What about Bob,* an extremely neurotic patient (Bill Murray) invades his psychiatrist's vacation home. Bob frustrates the doctor but is loved by Doc's family for his playfulness. In one scene, the doctor enters the kitchen to find the family having a blast doing dishes with Bob. They're all singing, and plates fly through the air from the person drying to the one putting dishes away. That's one way to make routine activities more fun, if your dishes survive!

Laundry play might be potentially less disastrous. My friend Barbara held Read 'n Fold "parties" with her daughters throughout their elementary-school years. They would read together nightly, and whenever clean clothes were pulled from the dryer, Barbara would have her girls fold clothes while she read to them. They read all the books in the Little House on the Prairie series, The Chronicles of Narnia, and Nancy Drew. (Yes, those are still around!)

ACTIVITIES YOU CHOOSE

Are you involved with any activities that seem necessary but might not be? Perhaps you know they aren't critical, but you feel you should do them? Activities we choose include:

- Volunteering (PTA, church, kids' clubs like Awana or Scouts)
- Political causes
- Employment to bring in additional but not critical income, to keep your career moving, or to build personal self-esteem
- Hobbies (scrapbooking, sewing, photography, etc.)
- Extracurricular activities for the kids (gymnastics, soccer, library programs)

Any of the above kinds of activities may be valuable to you. Just remember that you *do* choose them.

What's most important to you? Take a moment to consider your long- and short-term goals. Put them in order according to their level of importance to you at this time, considering your children's current ages. Here's my own list:

MY GOALS

Parenting
To grow closer to my children
To make my kids happy
To help my kids become responsible, productive, caring people
To help my children learn new things

Relationships
To nurture my marriage
To nurture relationships with extended family and friends
To show appreciation to those who help me
To help support my church, community, or children's schools

To nurture my personal faith and that of my children

Home
To keep my household running smoothly
To create a home I can be proud of
To prevent more work later

Work
To earn or save money to help buy necessities
To further my career
To earn money for luxuries and family fun

Health
To reduce stress in my life
To keep physically fit

Simplify Your Life

Make a list of all your current activities, noting alongside them why you're doing them. Do they fit one of your long- or short-term goals? Are you doing any activities simply because you were asked and couldn't say no?

Even activities you've deliberately chosen might not be the best use of your time when you have two goals at cross-purposes with each other. For instance, one year I volunteered to help at my middle child's elementary school. This met my goal of community involvement.

It was just a little job, working for a few hours a week to record calls from parents whose kids were ill. It would have been easy but for trying to keep my wiggly youngest child quiet so I could hear the phone messages. And although I was at my child's school, my goal of growing closer to my kids was not being met.

I finally realized that I could meet both goals by helping in Aimee's classroom periodically instead. Elisa enjoyed this as well.

Are you doing anything simply because you were asked and no one else seemed available? I hope you're not motivated to do activities by guilt, social pressure, fear of not being liked, fear of embarrassment, competitiveness, pride, or fear of not being considered a good parent. None of those are good reasons for choosing activities.

Can you let go of any current activities, perhaps even the goals that motivate them, without feeling guilty? Prioritize your goals and activities according to what is most important to *you* and *your family* at this time in your life. If you have a new baby, you should not expect to carry over all the volunteer activities you did before she was born. Even if your kids are older, consider dropping unnecessary activities that steal time you could spend with them.

You may feel very committed to volunteering in a specific area. But it is fine to take a hiatus while your children are small, with the intent of helping again in later years. This is especially important when a volunteer job doesn't merely take away family time but adds some element of stress.

When Aimee was small, I decided it was time to let go of a board position I held with a crisis organization helping domestic-violence and child-abuse victims. For about six years I'd volunteered as a crisis counselor, community educator, and volunteer trainer for the organization. Eventually it became difficult juggling child care so I could go to board meetings, and on occasion I was called to a woman in crisis at the same moment one of my own children had his or her own little crisis. I decided I needed to devote more time to my kids and could always volunteer again when they were older.

If you're an effective volunteer, other people may try to convince you that you're indispensable. This often happens when you've gained extensive knowledge and experience and others have come to depend on you. But if a position needs filling, someone *will* step up where you left off—perhaps someone who needs the experience or can even do a better job.

If possible, consider including your family in your volunteer work. This way, you can stay close with your kids while also teaching them some valuable lessons in the process. For instance, you might fill and deliver food baskets to the hungry at Christmas. Spend time visiting residents of a local nursing home or cleaning up a local park or playground. Gordy volunteers as an assistant teacher in Elisa's Sunday school class once a month. Be creative.

There are plenty of opportunities to help others and work together as a family at the same time.

JUGGLING WORK AND FAMILY

Decisions about your career can be difficult, especially if you've worked long and hard to get to a place you thought you wanted to be. You may have finally gotten that degree you worked so long and hard for—and paid so much for!—or have been offered a position you'd long hoped for.

It can take a long view and possibly some sacrifice to postpone, or even abandon, goals that were important to you B.C. (Before Children). Then again, many parents like myself have discovered parenthood to be so much more rewarding and powerful than they had imagined, making some previous career goals seem less meaningful. It can be worthwhile, if possible, to take a break from outside work to spend time with children or cut back on work hours.

I was hit very hard with this lesson when Aimee was a little over a year old. I was delighted to be swamped with writing assignments and to have the freedom to choose how much time I wanted to work. A college girl, Minda, was happy to baby-sit Aimee for me in the living room while I worked in my home office. Aimee loved her. I grew increasingly productive during the hours Tyler was away at school, and when he was home, I let the kids play together so I could catch up on housework.

I did think it a little peculiar that Aimee wasn't very snuggly with me. It seemed I had to beg for a kiss a little too often, even if she did giggle when running away. But I attributed that mostly to her busybody personality. I knew she loved me and was a happy child. She was fine. I was fine. We were all fine.

Then Minda left town to go back to school.

It had been a while since I'd lain on the floor just watching Aimee, doing little but letting her crawl all over me. To my complete dismay, within only a few days I realized that Minda had been getting a lot of those cuddles and kisses I had been missing. It nearly broke my heart.

That memory was so strong that years later, I was able to make a very difficult choice. Aimee was about three when a publisher was interested in having me write a book—this book, in fact. My dream come true! But when I was told I'd have to crank the project out within a year, I knew it would be a mistake to do it right then. I would miss Aimee's toddler and preschool years. So I came up with an alternate plan: I'd write the book piecemeal instead, in the form of magazine articles.

As you well know, life can be unpredictable. Shortly after meeting that editor, I found myself living in another country for two years and having a third child—whose toddlerhood I didn't want to miss either! Nevertheless, you hold the fruits of my long-term goal in your hands at this very moment.

I actually shudder to think how this project would have turned out had I actually done it eight years ago. What a blessing it has been to experience both the rewards and struggles with *three* children with entirely different personalities—and to continue to learn how to write well. What depth and richness my children have added to this project as they have grown older! There would be a big hole in this book without Elisa and her desire for a mother trophy. And there would be too much pride and naïveté on my part had I not had at least *one* child draw on a wall.

Please don't underestimate the lessons you will learn as a parent and the rewards of having children. Your destiny with your children is more far-reaching than you can imagine. The activities you choose to give up in order to make time for your children may well be replaced by family memories that will last for years to come.

What if you must work to help support your family? You can still make the most of the time you do have with your children, which probably will mean keeping life as simple as possible in other areas. You also may need to maximize what little time you have together. That's not easy when you are tired and must shift at the end of the day from work-related thinking to thinking about your child.

One single parent, Patty, has created a little ritual with her daughter to help make the transition from outside work to mothering easier. When she picks her five-year-old daughter, Julia, up at day care at the end of the day and they are riding home together, Julia teaches her mom new songs she has learned. Then they sing them together. Patty wishes she could spend more time with her daughter, yet she's got to pay the bills. To compensate, she spends as much time as she can playing on her days off and limits her outside activities for now.

PUT "PLAY" ON YOUR LIST

Limiting your outside activities won't necessarily make play happen. There's always more to running a home than most of us get around to doing. For some parents, unless library trips, swimming times, etc. are preplanned, they won't happen. One mom admitted to being perfectionistic about her housework, so she strongly felt the need to plan time for play. For instance, she planned time every day to read with her six- and three-year-old girls. However, she found she also needed to schedule times to simply take her girls by the hands and ask them, "What do you want to do?" (See Important Appointment, page 30.)

HOW MUCH IS ENOUGH?

Although you and your child will benefit from parent-child play, it's also important for your child to learn to play independently and for you to have some solitude as well.

You both need the intimacy that comes from playing together. But you also need time alone to clear your head, accomplish tasks, and be at peace. It is important, in the midst of chaotic parenting, to take time for yourself, to enjoy some adult conversation, perhaps to exercise or work on one of your hobbies.

I recall with amusement a children's book I read years ago. In the story, a mother elephant tried desperately to take a bath—of course, all her children wanted to join her. For a parent who is more solitary than social, this type of situation can present a real problem.

Your child should know that it's okay to play alone as well as with others. He needs to feel confident that he can entertain himself creatively—that he doesn't need you to regulate all his activities. It can be difficult to teach this to a dependent, social child, yet it can be done. (See sidebar on pages 48–49 for more ideas on independent play.)

How much play you and your child need is largely dependent on how playful your household is overall. I can't offer you a "play one hour per day" prescription. A lot of meaningful connecting can happen in passing: a quick tickle or "I'm gonna get you!" a spontaneous silly face, a quick spin to the music. Some days, that may be all the play you can squeeze in. Other days, your child may demand more, depending on her developmental level or how she feels that day, emotionally or physically.

But when too many days go by without play, stop and deliberately schedule a play break. Some of the most magical moments will only happen when you stop everything and focus deliberately on your child. You don't want all your parenting memories to be those of exhaustion and frustration. Take some time to create family memories of joy and intimacy to counterbalance that.

5 minute fun

ANIMAL ALPHABET

Take turns naming animals—but each new animal must begin with the last letter of the previous one (gira*ffe,* *e*lephan*t,* *t*iger, etc.). You'll soon begin to run out and will want to include fish, birds, and insects! You also may "outlaw" certain letters after a while (i.e., when *E* words are exhausted, outlaw animals ending in *E*.)

PANCAKE FUN

Keep a turkey baster in a drawer next to your stove. Once in a while, instead of making regular pancakes, squirt out alphabet shapes. Kids especially like getting their initials. This became a new art form when we photographed Wakako, our Japanese exchange student, writing her name with batter—in Japanese characters!

An alternative is smiley pancakes. First squirt the eyes, nose, and mouth into the pan and let them brown a little. Then use a measuring cup to pour a round pancake on top of the facial features and cook until done on both sides.

BABY BURGERS

Make a toddler-sized burger! Use a large drinking glass as a cookie cutter to cut a tot-sized bun after you've toasted it.

ONE-A-DAY SCAVENGER HUNT

If you must be away from your child for a few days, here's one way to play from afar. Purchase very cheap dollar-store items to hide around the house (or at Grandma's—wherever your child is staying). Leave a pile of notes, each one labeled for a day of the week you will be gone. The notes might say something like, "Today I am driving to Atlanta, and I already miss you!" Add secret instructions to help him find his prize for the day, such as: "Turn around three times, then clap your hands four times. Skip to the kitchen, open the food pantry, and look on the second shelf!" Call him later so he can excitedly tell you how he found the treasure you left him.

pampers to proms and beyond

Understanding Developmental Differences for Play at Any Age

Ah, the wonders of children—funny newborns, busily curious toddlers, blossoming preschoolers, analytical preteens. The more we play with them, the more we can marvel at their capabilities. Do you feel that awe?

I was laughing so hard I couldn't keep the video camera straight. But we still managed to record Gordy's antics with three-day-old Elisa. Holding her on his lap on my hospital bed, Gordy placed his thumb under her lower lip. He then moved it to make her "talk" as if she were a hand puppet. In a high voice, he said, "Boy has this been a rough day . . ."

He then "answered" her in his normal voice, "So what did you do today?"

He took her tiny finger and made her point it to her own head. Back to the high voice: "Um, let me think . . ." (Brother and sister giggle.) "I ate, slept, messed my diaper, ate, and slept again. What *is* that in your milk, Mom?" Our laughter drowned out much of what else our puppet said.

A few other mothers in the room, gently holding their swaddled infants, stared in disbelief as we unwrapped Elisa and tickled her awake so we could play with her.

In the Norwegian hospital where Elisa was born, moms typically stayed five days after a normal delivery. (Yes, it was lovely.) There were six mom-newborn couples in a room, dormitory style. Some had their first babies; a few had older children at home. But even to the experienced moms, I think we became known as "those crazy Americans." They may wonder to this day if all Americans make hand puppets out of their babies.

The truth is, we simply couldn't wait to play with our child. Admittedly, we didn't play with Tyler, our first child, at birth. We were too afraid he would *break*. I vividly remember wanting to see Tyler's hair when he was a few hours old, but Gordy kept covering the baby's head with a hat, worrying he'd be cold. Gordy also worried incessantly about keeping Tyler's head from wobbling. Looking at Elisa's video, it's amazing her head is still attached. Oh, we kept her safe enough—it just doesn't look like it, and we probably horrified my roomies.

When Elisa was one day old, she and I lay cheek to cheek listening to Vivaldi, sharing a pair of headphones. (Don't worry; I kept her earphone pulled gently away from her ear and the volume low.) I had played that music when I was pregnant and had reason to believe that recognizing it would be soothing to her.

But mostly, I wanted to share an intimate, beautiful moment with her—to take that new person in my life and have us do something special together, right away. My roommates also may have wondered why I spent so much time talking to my nonverbal baby as she lay propped on my bent knees in my hospital bed. They might even have wished that I would shut up so they could sleep. But being face-to-face and chatting with a baby is the earliest— and simplest—form of play.

DON'T LET APPEARANCES DECEIVE YOU

What's really interesting about watching video footage of Elisa's first week is seeing that she looked like any other newborn—jerky arms and legs, hands fisted, sleepy most of the time, eyes not focusing well. A sloppy, funny-looking little thing who looks as if she's not taking much in.

It truly looks as if everything we did to "play" with her was simply being done *to* her—for our entertainment, at her expense. In a sense, we were entertaining ourselves. We were having a blast with our new child, and she didn't have a clue about what we were doing. When she was our puppet, we were essentially playing with our older two children, using Elisa as a prop. (Of course, she now watches the video and thinks it's very funny.)

With newborns, it's not easy to see what kind of impact you're having. Although you can visibly see them calm down when you comfort them, talking to them may not seem to generate much response when they can't talk back and they're just getting used to focusing their eyes. Then again, if you look closely, you may be very surprised at how quickly your baby responds to you from the moment she is fresh out of the womb.

At about five hours old, Elisa lay on her stomach on my chest, her tiny head snuggled under my chin. Since it was the middle of the night, our room was darkened except for a small light by the bed. Wide awake, I talked to my baby. Shakily, she raised her head up and our eyes locked. Her head flopped back down, whew . . . then up again, to stare deeply into my eyes. At that moment a fly buzzed by (don't ask me why it was in the hospital) and angrily hit the light. With jerky movements, Elisa turned her head to watch the fly and stared at it until it flew away. Newborns *do* respond to sights and sounds, although they often lack the motor skills, words, and facial expressions to show us. (In this instance, she did respond using motor skills.)

I have a most intriguing photograph, taken on day five of Elisa's life. Just before our release from the hospital, four of us mom-baby pairs posed for the shot. The three other moms stood in identical positions, babies swaddled and cradled in their arms. I, crazy American, held Elisa upright and facing the camera, her arms dangling out, her blanket falling off. And remarkably, she is *looking* at the camera! Her bright brown eyes are focused directly on the person taking the picture.

The significance of that photo is not so much how alert she looked but how it demonstrated my attitude towards her. I simply assumed that she would want to see what was going on. She was another person in the picture, and I wanted her face in it, not the blanket! I held her up because I wanted her involved in everything we were doing—including picture-taking—and she responded.

DON'T WAIT TO PLAY

I believe that kids are interested in life from birth on; they're people put into our lives to interact with us from the start. This belief affects the way I behave with them. This goes beyond basic care, although some of our most interactive moments happen when we diaper or feed babies. With newborns, you must look beyond uncontrolled movements and grimaces to see little clues that your baby is aware of what's happening around her. But instead of waiting until a baby reacts to start playing with him, consider this: Your interaction may teach him how to respond!

I appreciate what Michael A. Weiford, Mental Health Program Director and child specialist for The Center for Counseling and Health Resources, has to say about this. He says he can tell by talking to older children just how much their parents have interacted with them.

"If a child has a very enthusiastic parent, one who initiates play, that child is probably going to look more interactive, early on." He says this is often apparent in the way the child makes eye contact with other adults. When babies experience eye contact and watch adults making faces, they learn to echo back those expressions. Here's a fascinating example: Kathy, a forty-five-year-old mother, was delighted when her eldest child married, then had a newborn. But when she saw her grandchild, her face could not fully express her joy. You see, half of her face is temporarily paralyzed due to the recent removal of a brain tumor. Yet, when Kathy smiled her crooked smile at the infant, the baby smiled back— with an equally crooked smile!

My brother Frank and his wife, Sim, were thrilled at the birth of their newborn, despite a traumatic delivery. And their baby immediately got the full range of smiles and cuddles. But like most new parents, they had the usual nervousness about how to bathe, diaper, and dress a new baby. (Gordy and I had been just as nervous with our first child. I equate stuffing a newborn's arms and legs into a sleeper with trying to push cooked spaghetti noodles through a straw!)

Frank and Sim also had the usual worries about understanding their baby's different cries and about his poop being the right color and consistency. Top that off with the lack of sleep, complicated by my sister-in-law's recovery from a painful delivery, and other than cuddling with baby Eli and cooing at him, *playing* with him no doubt seemed premature.

Thankfully, I'd had lots of practice with my own babies, so when I flew to see baby Eli when he was six weeks old, I was ready to *play*.

Upon my arrival my brother pointed to his son lying in the bassinet and asked, "So when can we expect some action?"

"Right *now!*" I couldn't wait to get my hands on that child. I propped my nephew on my knees as we sat on the couch, and we began a conversation. When the baby was *goo*ing back at me and smiling, and my brother spoke to me, I said, "Excuse me, but you are interrupting our conversation!"

That no doubt sounded goofy. If it was like most of my conversations with little ones, the baby probably said, "Goo" and I answered, "Is that *right?* Tell me more!" To his smile, leg kicks, and "Ahuaa gah" I answered with disbelief, "No way! You've got to be kidding!"

At some point I usually throw in an "I'm gonna get you!" with a gentle surprise tickle afterward. After enough repetitions, a baby learns that it's coming, begins to smile, then—as my nephew did—to giggle. Ah, that first, musical, lovely, charming giggle. What a joyful sound! It's really the anticipation of the tickle that brings the laugh—and at six weeks a baby can quickly learn, anticipate, and respond to the tickle game.

Yes, the "action" often begins long before that first giggle. However, my brother's expectations were not unusual. In a recent survey, 62 percent of 1,066 parents responded "Two months or older" to the question "At what age do you think an infant or young child begins to really take in and react to the world around them?" That was even if the interviewer clarified the question by adding, " . . . meaning the child takes in the sights, sounds, and smells of the surroundings and reacts to them?"[9]

I suspect that this misconception is most common among parents of first babies, who find that caring for an infant's basic needs can be overwhelming. And yet many of those same parents might be astonished at how simple it is to entertain a baby and stimulate that little brain.

If you have a newborn, talk to her, sing to her as much as you can. Get her into a position where she can see as much *action* as possible—in an infant seat, slightly propped up on the dining-room table, or on a blanket on the floor. The stimulation you provide your baby actually helps build new connections in his brain, firing off in rapid succession, building from one to another. The physical mechanics of this were described in a *Time* magazine article that reviewed fascinating research done by neurologists studying infant brains.[10]

Little Eli, although not quite able to grab anything yet, was immediately interested when Sim and I dangled toys from the bar of his infant seat. At first he just looked at them with interest and jerked his arms with excitement. But within days he was attempting to bat at them with jerky arms and clenched fists.

If you assume your newborn is interested in everything you do, mundane chores take on new meaning. Why merely fold laundry when you can play peekaboo with your baby using a dishtowel? Within a few months, he'll put it on his own head and sit there waiting expectantly for you to pull it off!

Why change his sleeper silently—unless that's all you can muster in the middle of the night—when you can say, "Hmm . . . do you want the *blue* or the *yellow* one today? See the bear on this one? Okay, in goes *one* leg, now *two*. Oh! I'd better kiss those little toes, first!" *Smooch!*

Is he spending too much time laying flat on his back looking at a designer mobile that doesn't even hang so *he* can see the designs? Try taping colorful posters to the ceiling above your baby's crib and pictures on the wall alongside the changing table. You can use black-and-white swirly drawings made by preschool siblings or magazine ads with smiling faces or cartoon characters—basically anything with color or contrast.

As my kids grew, I continued to try to see through their eyes. Yesterday I came across a poster of a bunny I'd forgotten about entirely, taped to the underside of our dining-room table. It's a lovely little memento of fleeting infant playtimes—when my crawling babies loved to hide out there. I think I'll leave it there to find by accident again sometime.

TODDLERS

Like newborns, toddlers are often underestimated. By your child's second birthday, you probably will have seen your jerky newborn grow into a child who not only can sit up but can walk forward and backward, even upstairs, and run without falling. She jumps in place—landing on both feet—and can throw and kick a ball. What a lot of physical milestones in such a short amount of time!

As for fine motor skills, also by age two, she's probably building a block tower and holding a crayon in her fist to scribble in her high chair. She's likely to enjoy taking pegs in and out of a board and turning book pages as you read to her.[11]

Communication begins early, even without words. A one-year-old can make it very clear what he does or does not want. He can even learn a little sign language. Elisa learned the motion for the word *more* and consistently used it when in her high chair. One day, at a grocery store offering free samples, I turned my back on her for a few seconds as she sat in the cart. I turned back to see her making the "more" sign in *giant* motions. (She was yelling it, you see, so I could hear her better!)

Lately when I'm on the phone with my brother, it delights me to hear toddler Eli giggling in the background as he pounces on his daddy's stomach while Frank tries to talk to me. I love it when my brother interrupts himself and fades away from the phone, saying, "Yeah, Eli, ball! Ball!" then tells me how much his baby loves balls and tries to remember where we were in our conversation. I just wish I could *see* them romping together.

Meanwhile, a toddler understands hundreds of words, even when she's not yet speaking. I recall being startled when three-year-old Tyler pointed and said, "That's a Frisbee—like I played with with Uncle Frank." Indeed he had, at eighteen months old—the only time he'd ever seen his uncle or a Frisbee. Aimee, at eighteen months old, was not yet talking. But one day she startled me by suddenly running to fetch me a broom; she'd overheard me muttering to myself that the floor needed sweeping. I recall wondering, *When did she equate the word* sweep *with a broom?*

As words come, toddlers can combine the few they know with other methods of communication. When Elisa was a tiny tot, she came running into the kitchen gesturing wildly.

"Aaa!" she cried out. "A eebeebidoh, my woom!"

"What's an eebeebidoh?" I asked.

That tiny thing sighed, rolled her eyes, then sang, in tune, the following, complete with hand motions: "Eebee, eebeebidoh, ubba wadda bowt. Uh uh uh wain, uh, wassa bidah out." Then she grabbed my hand, and dragged me to her room to get rid of that itsy bitsy spider on her wall!

Unfortunately, when immobile babies become mobile toddlers, parents often lose enthusiasm about their children's curiosity.

A Comedy of Errors

I had whipped the kitchen into shape: the counters were bare (a miracle), the floor was mopped. Toddler Elisa was bathed and dressed in freshly laundered clothes, her hair washed—was I on a roll or what?

Then I turned to find her sitting on the floor, covered from head to toe with the contents of a supersized container of chocolate-milk powder, which she'd tried to "drink." Four cups of brown powder clumped into her wet hair, onto her clean clothes, and all over my shiny floor. It was enough to make a mother cry. But on this occasion, I ran for the video camera.

Why?

Well, she did look pretty funny, especially due to the shocked look on her face. Also, it all seemed rather unreal. Only a few days before, we'd videotaped a previous disaster. I had heard her crying in the bathroom and found her naked, standing in the tub. My independent child had decided to "wash" her own hair—using the entire contents of a supersized bottle of baby shampoo and without a single drop of water in the tub. Getting it all out created an unbelievable amount of suds—so many that they filled the tub and I had to transfer my slippery child to the shower in the other bathroom!

Amazingly, between the soapsuds and the chocolate powder, my sense of humor had remained intact. That was despite the fact that cleanup stole time I'd rather have spent doing something else!

But alas, I finally did lose my patience when I found my independent and creative child in my clothes closet. She was using my face makeup and lipstick as art mediums, and my carpet as a canvas. Now, I must confess, I was really angry about this. Perhaps my hormones had finally hit their midmonth stride, but I was *seriously* upset. When Gordy ran in with the video camera to catch all that cuteness on film, I wanted to slug him and told him to put it away. He chuckled and kept it rolling.

Knowing that I was being recorded forced me to take deeper breaths and lower my tone of voice. Oh, it's still clear on film that I was not a happy camper—those stains never did come out of the carpet, even after an hour of scrubbing. (Help, Heloise?) But perhaps we all need a camera in our face when we're upset with our children, so we might consider more thoughtfully how to react.

Looking on the bright side, we rarely entertain guests in the closet. And that run of three experiments remained just that—no major incidents after that at all! Thankfully, Elisa did learn from her mistakes, so now they're just funny stories.

If your life is currently full of supersized messes, you may wish that toddlerhood would pass quickly. Sure enough, it will. But remember, within just a three-year period, your child will go from crawling to walking to talking. The explosion in language is phenomenal. In that short amount of time, your child will progress from saying, "Miwk" and pointing to the refrigerator to saying, "Mom, can I have some milk on my cereal?" She may even retrieve it and pour it herself!

Try to remember to write down evidence of your child's curiosity that reveals his personality or what he is learning. It can be truly fascinating if you take time to think about why she's doing what—there's often a very rational reason.

Why did she throw your unpaid bills in the garbage? Because she's seen you toss opened envelopes there. Why did she dip the toothbrush in the toilet? Perhaps to her, it's a child-sized toilet-bowl brush—and she's "helping"! Is he imitating the screech of seagulls or lifting up your shirt to tickle you? clicking his tongue while trying to snap his fingers? pushing the redial button on your phone and jabbering in his own strange language to a confused listener on the other end? (This comes in handy when telemarketers call. Hand the phone to your tot!)

PRESCHOOL TO EARLY ELEMENTARY

During an evening car ride, three-year-old Tyler and I saw the full moon, partially obscured by clouds. He pointed at it and yelled excitedly, "Wow, look at that filthy moon!" My child's comment gave me a chance to peek into his mind. I could "see" him processing new information and attempting to organize it in a meaningful way.

Small children tend to perceive life differently from grown-ups. How? Well, for starters, your preschooler is likely to observe things more closely than you do. What we classify as mundane or ordinary often fascinates young children. That fascination can give you a chance to look at life with fresh eyes, helping you to appreciate things you've grown too busy to notice. When your child sees something he wants to show you, allow some time to stop and look at it closely with him.

Also, keep in mind that your child at this age is a munchkin stuck in a giant world. Can you imagine how tiresome it must be to not be able to see over the top of counters and to always be looking adults in the knees or the navel? No wonder kids often enjoy playing with miniatures like Fisher-Price dolls or kid-sized items like play kitchens or small plastic power tools. No wonder Elisa recently cried out with excitement and pride, "Mom! I can reach this cupboard now. I'm getting *bigger!*" One children's book by Mercer Mayer, *When I Get Bigger,* [12] has been a big hit with all three of my kids.

A small child is also often focused on attempts to master his body. Kids often need special encouragement in this area, because they rarely can make their body do what they want it to on the first try. Learning to crawl, walk, use the toilet, catch a ball, or walk a balance beam all require practice. Unfortunately, if your child experiences a lot of failure and not much encouragement, he may begin to avoid some physical activities. If you go on walks together, you can help him practice moving his body. You can be silly, walking like penguins or hopping like kangaroos. Who cares if the neighbor thinks you're weird? Be extra patient when your child insists on *slowly* walking logs or concrete barriers, even if you're in a hurry and en route somewhere. At home, try patting your heads and rubbing your tummies at the same time.

Little ones also enjoy "exercising" their senses. Their sense of touch is stimulated when they play with finger paints or Play-Doh. You might also try "What's in the bag?" and ask your child to close his eyes and guess what objects are in a paper sack, simply by using his sense of touch. Of course, hugs can be added freely to just about any activity you do with your child. Incidentally, I typed in "hugs per day" on the Web and saw a general consensus that four hugs per day are necessary for good health, with eight to twelve hugs being optimal! As for the other four senses, children love to practice using their eyes with games like I Spy, in which one person chooses an object in the room and the other person has to guess the object by asking questions ("Is it blue? Is it shiny?"). They like to practice using their ears by listening to classical or jazz music to pick out instrument sounds. And it's fun to stimulate their senses of taste

and smell by "playing" in the kitchen—baking chocolate chip cookies together with Mom or Dad, or guessing spices by scent.

Another thing small children struggle with (many adults do
too) is understanding what they are feeling, why they feel that
way, and how to express that. It helps to identify feelings as your
child exhibits them (e.g., "You must feel proud of yourself for finishing that puzzle"). You can also play games about feelings; for
instance, take turns identifying facial expressions (each other's
and those of people in magazine advertisements). You can also
say, "Tell me about . . ." Ask your child to describe something he
thinks is funny, embarrassing, or weird. To get your child to tell
you about his day, ask him if anything made him angry, unhappy,
excited, or happy that day at preschool.

Your child's feelings often include ambivalence about growing
up. One moment she wants to be the boss, the next moment, the
baby. Growing up can be scary—all that new responsibility!
Unfortunately, very young children think we know their
thoughts—that we *know* how they want to be treated at any
given moment. But we often don't. When our kids' words or
behavior indicates they are feeling ambivalent about growing up,
we need to accept those feelings and help them deal with them.
You might let your child temporarily pretend he's a baby again,
once in a while. Or you can tell him about funny words he used
when he was a baby and look at his baby pictures together. If he
has a sibling who is a baby, talk about some of the neat things he
can do that the baby can't yet.

Lastly, keep in mind that small children have active imagina-
tions. At times they need help sorting out what is real and what
isn't. Pretending is a large part of a small child's world. Our job as
parents isn't always to draw them back to reality. The world of pretend serves a vital function to a child. In playing "pretend," children experiment with adult roles and practice social skills; it helps
them take our adult world and make sense of it. You can pretend
together with toy animals or puppets. Play dress up and take photos. It's also fun to use a pretend cash register and play store with
plastic food, books, or toys.

Enjoy the preschool age while it lasts! Try to write down the funny ways your child talks (including how he or she speaks, phonetically). Write down your child's favorite activities even if you think you won't forget them—you may.

LATE ELEMENTARY AND BEYOND

You might be surprised at how long you can continue to play preschool games with older kids. Just when you think they've outgrown a game, they'll ask for it again or initiate it with a younger sibling. Kids of all ages like to make super-duper living-room-sized blanket forts.

Even reading aloud is something you don't want to abandon too early. Sixth-grade Aimee still likes to read books with me, and we alternate reading chapters. Sometimes the person doing the reading gets a marvelous arm massage, so I often insist on a longer turn!

But as kids get older, it is fun to be able to play more sophisticated games. I love to play Cribbage, a card game with a special board with pegs, partly because I remember my own daddy teaching me how to play, and partly because it's exciting to see older kids figure out the math strategies involved.

Depending on their personalities, you can also get children to participate in some of your favorite hobbies with you. Gordy and Tyler enjoy skiing, and the girls and I love to scrapbook. Although Elisa still needs help gluing photos down, Aimee now creates such beautiful pages that I'm beginning to look to *her* for advice!

It can be surprising and delightful when a child independently gravitates towards an activity you enjoy yourself. When Aimee was about eight, I found some little stories she had entered into our computer on her own. I told her how it excited me to see that she and I share the same interest. She looked at me with a puzzled expression, then she said, "Oh. You mean you like to write too?" (I'd taken a break from writing when Elisa was an infant and toddler.)

With big kids, aside from doing hobbies together, I think the best way to play is to enjoy a general atmosphere of playfulness. Older children develop a more mature sense of humor, which can be very fun. You can share with them the latest *Reader's Digest* jokes at the dinner table; they understand them and can laugh with you.

It's not easy, of course, when kids begin to hit puberty. One mother I knew in Norway, Turunn, described a long-standing family tradition of playing cards and other competitive games as a family once a week. But as her three girls became teenagers, they began to shun those game nights with Mom and Dad. Friends, even the TV, were more interesting. Turunn also complained that their play atmosphere at that time was affected by her thirteen-year-old's moodiness—she acted grown-up in some ways and rather childish in others. It can be tricky navigating those hormonal waters. You must feel your way, day by day, thinking creatively about how to playfully interact with your child who is turning into a young adult—a child who has long outgrown peekaboo but still needs some cuddles.

Yes, we need to let our kids grow up. But we need not let go of all our old playful ways.

GROWN-UP PLAY

Hopefully the playfulness you model throughout your children's lives will carry over for them into their adult lives. Gordy and I are not only playful with our children; we're playful with each other. In fact, that's a big thing that attracted me to him. Once (before we were married) we were temporarily separated when I went to New Mexico as an exchange student for three months. Gordy had gone home to New Jersey. Not long afterward, I received an unusual care package from him. I opened it to find a box of dead leaves!

He'd been feeling sad that in the desert I was missing seeing glorious fall colors, so my beloved had sent me a season. (Awww.) Although the reds and golds had faded, the package also contained hilarious instructions. I was to throw the leaves in the air over my head, with a fan blowing, to appreciate the full effect of autumn. He has continued throughout our marriage to surprise me with playful, creative surprises—even when midlife doldrums threaten to steal playfulness.

I hope we retain that for a lifetime and that our kids do as well. I still remember the day my ninety-five-year-old grandma Gladys chuckled and said, "I used to play basketball, you know, back in the 1920s. In fact, I still do! I *roll* up my dirty laundry and *shoot* it into the bathtub!"

TODDLER READING FUN
Instead of boring yourself by reading only board books designed just for babies or toddlers, keep on the lookout for picture books with beautiful drawings, even if they have a lot of text. Let your child point to the pictures and simply say the names of objects, or ask him to find things for you in the pictures. Read every single day, and your child will learn how to treat books. Teach babies that books are precious, never to be ripped or chewed on.

When your child can handle listening to a sentence per page (at about eighteen months), make up your own condensed version as you turn the pages. Sometimes you can eliminate every other sentence and the story still makes sense. Or you can simply make up your own story, using the pictures as a guide. As you read, don't be afraid to use big words with little people. Often, with the pictures and context of the story, the child can understand what they mean.

BOMBS AWAY!
When was the last time you had a water fight with your kids on a hot summer day? Although I tend to stay out of the fray—I mean spray— Gordy can really get into it with the kids. Water balloons, squirt guns, the garden hose—whatever squirts or splashes becomes ammo. I stay dry inside, videotaping the battle through the windows!

DAIRY QUEEN BINGO
If you can get your hands on bingo cards, an evening of Bingo can entertain kids from elementary age through high school—plus their friends—when played with this special twist: With each round, the prize for winning escalates. Start with a plain vanilla cone, then escalate to a sundae with fudge sauce, then up the ante even further to a full-fledged banana split. After playing, you can all take off for DQ to get what you've "won." (*Contributed by Valerie Crockett*)

but we're so different!

Understanding How Personality Affects Play

Your child is distinct. Unique. Do you know him?

Can you understand what drives her? Can you find

more patience, more joy, more desire to play with

and get to know each precious person put

in your life by grand design?

Before age two, Elisa cried when she saw photos of places she'd not yet been, especially family-vacation photos we had taken before she was born. By two and a half, she declared that when she got bigger, she would scale the REI climbing rock and go hot-air ballooning (although no one else in the family ever had). I have no doubt that when Elisa is bigger, spying some wild, exotic place in *National Geographic,* she'll catch the next flight out. Heaven help her poor mother, whose idea of adventure is working on photo albums.

Elisa has also always planned physical movements with precision and seriousness—for instance, repeatedly working to perfect a headstand-back arch combo off the footrest, despite never having been exposed to gymnastic lessons. The Olympics on television fascinated her at age three, and she began calling an old bike-parade ribbon her "gold medal." I recently saw with some dismay that she has blisters on her hands. When I asked her why, she shrugged and said it's from practicing on the rings on the preschool playground.

Where does personality come from? Is there an adventure gene? a gymnastics gene?

Not really, but we *are* born with certain temperamental qualities. How you raise your child will affect his personality. But much of what makes your child who he is exists from birth on—and even in utero.

Psychologists and behavioral scientists have varied opinions about how such traits come to us in the first place. An evolutionary bias assumes we inherit certain recognizable traits and genetic patterns somewhat by default. A creationist bias assumes that we are designed with a grand plan in mind, by a loving Creator. To be honest, I find hope and promise in assuming that God made us on purpose, for the fun of it—that he sorted your genes, my genes, and our children's genes "just so."

Regardless of your opinion about how you and your child received your remarkably differing DNA patterns—even your spit is different!—you must live with those inherited temperamental qualities. Sometimes that's not easy! But when you see children as individuals, brimming with great potential and a unique purpose for their lives, it's easier to be more understanding about differences. It can help us to be more tolerant and encouraging.

I found it useful early on as a parent to learn about, and begin identifying, common inborn traits. Many fun and interesting personality tests and labels have stemmed from the identification of such traits. Gary Smalley, in his children's book *The Treasure Tree,* reveals four basic personality types in the form of animals: a playful otter, an organized beaver, a take-charge lion, and a sensitive golden retriever. The lovely pictures in that book and the fun story line make it a good read with children. Kids seem to enjoy trying to figure out what animal they are most like—and they are often right on target.

However, I think that more important than giving a child a label or trying to plug him in to a specific personality type is considering what motivates him. Correcting, teaching, guiding, playing—all are easier done when you understand what a child most craves. Is it orderliness and structure? relationships? spontaneity? taking charge? Even the way you apply consequences to misbehavior works best if chosen in light of inborn tendencies. An extroverted socialite is miserable after five minutes in time-out. A child who most craves control—and may need time to recharge by being alone—may defiantly refuse to come out long after you tell him he can!

Although personality typing is fascinating, in the context of this book it will be most helpful to get back to the basics—identification of common inborn traits. Stella Chess, M.D., and Alexander Thomas, M.D., were pioneers in this area of research, focusing on what they called the "goodness of fit" between parent and child. They found that fit is affected by the following common traits:

- Persistence and focus
- Short attention spans and distractibility
- Sensory threshold
- Activity level (high or low)
- Mood and intensity of responses
- Approach or withdrawal (to new situations, people, toys) and adaptability (long-term reactions)
- Regularity (regular, or irregular, sleeping and eating patterns, etc.)

In their book, *Know Your Child,* they linked these traits to the ways in which children, from birth on, act and react—and how parents relate to them. That book helped me see early on what made my first child "tick." I was then amused and amazed at how different the second two children were.

Let's examine each trait in detail, considering the effects of each trait on parent-child play. As you learn more about your kids, you'll be able to plan more successful activities, lessen potential for "disaster" during the course of play, and have a whole lot more fun together.

PERSISTENCE AND FOCUS

Chess and Thomas describe persistence as "the continuation of an activity in the face of obstacles or difficulties."[13]

Let's look at a cluster of traits commonly grouped with persistence and the ability to focus well. One trait is the *compulsion to finish tasks*. This is usually linked to a *long attention span,* sometimes complicated by *perfectionism.* Quite often, a child with these traits also possesses a strong sense of *justice,* a high level of *competitiveness,* and possibly a very strong will *(determination)*.

You may have a child who possesses a few of these traits—or all of them. These traits are all admirable under the right circumstances, but they also can cause battles.

Compulsion for Completion

A persistent child often feels compelled to finish what he's started. He may worry about missing something and feel frustrated if he's forced to quit in the middle of play. My son once cried because he "couldn't see the whole movie"—when he missed a single ending credit. We were left standing alone in the theater, to my great impatience!

A persistent child may become angry if, when playing, you've had enough, but he hasn't. You think, *Good grief, didn't he appreciate the time we spent together already?* He may resent having to drop an activity to come to dinner, especially if he's also slow to adapt and not easily distracted. It helps to give a child like this reasonable time warnings and a moment to develop a plan for when to finish the project.

Let's say your daughter is working on a puzzle. You can help her by saying, "I like your persistence in wanting to finish this puzzle, but in five minutes you have to stop so we can eat dinner. How about finishing the elephant's head? Then, after dinner, you can do the rest."

This allows the child some sense of completion and gives her a moment to detach from what she's so intent on. As adults, we often don't think about how *we* would feel if we were engrossed in an activity and told without a moment's notice to stop. Time warnings help everyone make smoother transitions, but they're especially helpful with an intense or compulsive child.

Interestingly enough, even if a child, through his own actions, cuts an activity short (as my son did by scattering the Memory cards [see chapter 2]), he may still feel angry about not getting to finish playing.

Long Attention Span

In conjunction with persistence, some children possess a long attention span, sticking with activities for a long time without interruption. This attribute is a true blessing, unless your child is playing with someone else who becomes easily bored or distracted and wants to change activities (perhaps yourself?).

Under these circumstances, it requires some forethought to choose an activity that everyone present can enjoy, yet one that can be cut short with a minimum of frustration. For example, Monopoly (unless you adapt it in the ways I suggest on page 156) will feel unfinished if you simply stop in the middle. I Spy, on the other hand, can be played until you feel like quitting. If your child consistently likes to do activities longer than you or a friend of his does, it helps to frankly discuss that with him. Tell him you appreciate this part of his personality (his ability to stick with things) but the play date is a time to enjoy the people he is with as well. You might be surprised at how well he understands this. He will help you choose activities that are most fun with a particular parent, friend, or sibling.

But be careful. It's easy to devote less time and energy—including playtime—to a child who sticks with projects or reads for hours independently than you would to a distractible child. This can create a sharp contrast if you are constantly attending to a busy brother or sister. Even if you aren't playing but simply keeping Little Brother out of trouble, Big Sister may feel slighted even if she appears to be occupied and hasn't specifically asked for attention.

Being open with your child about this situation will help. If your younger child is a constant distraction, you may need to make "dates" with your older child so he can truly have you to himself for a while.

Perfectionism

A persistent child may also demand high quality and attention to detail, making him intolerant of his own or other's mistakes. A child putting together a model car with Mom may feel exasperated when he can't get the dashboard sticker on straight and asks for help. When Mom doesn't do any better, he gets mad at her, too. Mom, annoyed, thinks he's overreacting—the sticker looked fine in the first place, for heaven's sake. And why is this child so unappreciative of her help? This may result in an angry retort like, "Do it yourself, then!"

Perfectionism may cause a child to stubbornly beg to do something, or have something, or go somewhere, that's not practical, wise, or fun for you. She may get "locked in" to redoing something until it's right, fussing and fuming all the while. Your fun project of making valentines may disintegrate when a child keeps recutting hearts to get one just right. If she misspells a word on the completed valentine, she may insist tearfully that now it's "ruined" and she must redo the whole thing. It can be frustrating to try to persuade her otherwise.

It does appear that in firstborn children this tendency is sometimes more pronounced. Perhaps this is because firstborns tend to compare themselves to adults instead of other children. Telling a child you have thirty years of experience, while he has only five, doesn't necessarily help.

This trait is also very common in intellectually gifted children. They may struggle when they have strong desires to achieve what an older child or adult can do but don't yet have the fine- or large-motor capabilities to do so. My son, at age four, wrote a letter to a friend about his newborn baby sister. I was dismayed when he shredded the completed letter upon discovering that he'd formed one alphabet letter incorrectly. (Thankfully, I taped the letter back together and photocopied it, so I still have that delightful letter.)

Telling a child like this that he doesn't really need to know how to write yet anyway will make no difference. The good news is that perfectionistic tendencies can be decreased dramatically. I think children need reassurance that imperfection is often okay—and that we learn from failures as well as successes. At times I wondered if decreasing perfection was good . . . when I had to wade through discarded clothing and candy wrappers on my child's bedroom floor to kiss him good-night. Now, however, he has a new, teen-friendly room, and he's keeping it amazingly clean.

Justice

Persistence and a long attention span often come with a strong sense of justice, in which a child feels that all games must be played the "right" way. He may cry, "Unfair!" when changes are made to accommodate differing abilities or be inflexible about playing a game in a new way. It is possible to change rules and make adaptations, but with a child like this it is critical to talk this out before the game starts.

Sometimes putting one child in the role of teacher instead of competitor (*before* starting a game, not in the midst of it) increases the chances that the activity together will be successful. For example, had I talked with Tyler before our Memory game, showed him how I had helped him learn it when he was younger, and reminded him that his sister had never played, we could have made a deal of some sort. We might have agreed for him to teach her in one game, then play a "real" one with me later. Had he, right off the bat, seen himself aligned *with* me as a coteacher, instead of *against* me, unfairly matched against a sister who was receiving special help, he would have felt more tolerant of her ability level.

Competitiveness

A more competitive spirit can take the fun out of games when worries about winning take over. This can be especially tricky when a child truly hopes to beat you at a table game, but your age and experience make it unlikely that she will. If you try to secretly let her win and she knows it, you may offend her, with her preoccupation with justice and fairness. If she doesn't win, it may sour her mood. Unless you plan to openly teach her, your best bet is probably to engage in a noncompetitive game or activity.

Of course, with competitive activities you have the opportunity to teach your child to be nongloating and gracious when he wins, as well as accepting and cheerful when he loses.

One day when Elisa and I were playing a table game, she suddenly realized that with my next move I would win the game. She glowered at me, jumped down, ran to her room, slammed her door, and refused to speak to me.

After a few minutes I came in and sat on her bed.

I asked her, "Do you think you should win every time, and I should lose every time?" She looked a little uncertain. Then she revealed a hint of a smile and said, "Yes!"

"Hmm," I continued. "Does beating me at a game make you a better person than me? Or does my beating you make me a better person than you?"

Now she looked really uncertain. "Uh . . . no," she said.

"Sometimes I'll win, and sometimes you will. But we can still have fun together, can't we?"

At that, she either caught on or was simply tired of our discussion. She jumped up, pulled my arm, and said, "Can we go play something else now?"

Determination

Often called "stubborn" or "strong willed," a determined child can give parents a truly rough time. This can happen not only in areas regarding discipline but also in the course of play. Your child will need to learn and practice negotiating skills so that he doesn't alienate others by insisting that they always play his way.

You may also feel mixed emotions if you struggle with stubbornness yourself. Playing together may be a bit like two mountain goats butting heads.

One mom, Lisa, says a sitter once told her, "Your daughter is *so* stubborn!" to which Lisa responded, "How *dare* you label my baby! She's only seven months old!" But she, too, had already seen that stubborn streak from day one, when her baby refused to be fed or held by others.

Says Lisa, "It was hard to think about my daughter being labeled this way, because *I* was stuck with that label as a child. I didn't mean to be a problem. I just had strong feelings about the way things should be." She sees her daughter now, age ten, struggling with friendships because of her stubbornness—oops, I mean determination!

However, Lisa does see the positive side to her daughter's determination. Like Lisa, she is a leader, enjoys being up front, and is outgoing. Those attributes enabled Lisa to avoid drugs and other temptations as a teen and helped her build a successful business as a consultant and public speaker.

Sometimes a child who is normally persistent may surprise you by a lack of determination in an area in which he's not as strong. A child who masters intellectual tasks easily and is used to instant success may give up too soon on a physically demanding activity that does not come as easily. If you see this tendency in your child, remind him that repeated attempts and failures are often part of learning and discovery.

Remember the Positive

If you haven't guessed already, persistence, a strong sense of justice, and competitiveness all contributed to my son's seemingly irrational reaction during our Memory game. But at sixteen years old, he's able to use those same qualities to help him achieve a level of independence and thoroughness in independent school projects that is truly astounding.

Because of his high level of persistence, he's a lot of fun to play games with, now that his persistence is coupled with more maturity. At fifteen, he engaged me in a game of Risk that lasted, believe it or not, about six hours. After midnight we were droopy eyed and rolling the dice with limp hands. But we were having too much fun to stop. Noncompetitive me would normally have given up and hit the sheets, but it was a joy to be with my son, especially now that he spends more and more time with friends. And along with his persistence comes his dry, witty sense of humor, which made me laugh to the point of tears during that midnight Risk game.

Yes, high persistence can often create conflict during play. But think again about those related tendencies. A strong sense of justice. An urge to finish what is started. A demand for high quality. Attention to detail. An unwillingness to give up. Wow. Those qualities don't sound so bad, do they?

To me, they paint a portrait of a highly successful adult—assuming that there is a balance. It is advantageous for a businessperson or an athlete to be competitive—but not at the expense of others. Attention to quality and finishing what is started makes someone productive and dependable, as long as she isn't too hard on herself or others. This world needs justice and fairness—balanced with understanding and compassion. If your child's persistence drives you crazy sometimes, remind yourself of these positive aspects, and spend time praying for her—and nurturing her spiritual life as well as her intellectual life.

SHORT ATTENTION SPANS AND DISTRACTIBILITY

A child with low persistence and a short attention span often gives up on activities quickly. This is a problem if you've invested a lot of yourself in preparing for that activity—perhaps going to great lengths to set up a game or craft (at your child's request!)—which she then abandons too quickly.

Let's say your child has begged to play with Play-Doh. You get out dough and cookie cutters. You cover the carpet with protective plastic. Five minutes after the materials are scattered around the table and floor, your child wants to play Go Fish instead. You spend another ten minutes putting materials away.

To reduce frustration, it helps to make preparation and cleanup part of the activity—even a game in itself. As your child becomes more responsible and independent, he may learn to consider whether or not an activity is worth the prep time to *him*.

You can also reduce your frustration by being more aware of your child's attention limits and choosing activities accordingly. You can also help your child by encouraging him to be more persistent. You don't want him to give up too easily on something you know he can master with some practice, something he would ultimately enjoy. Praising him for persistence, even in the midst of failure, helps. "I know you keep falling off your bike. But it's great to see you keep trying! I *know* you can do it. Hey, pretty soon we'll be riding bikes together!"

If your child is not terribly concerned with quality, but you are, it may take effort to resist pointing out errors during playtimes together. Remind yourself that your goal is to enjoy your playtime together and to grow closer. This has to be balanced with helping your child to grow, learn, and achieve something he or she will proud of. So at times you might try to persuade your child to spend a little more time and effort on something, encouraging him to see the benefits.

Distractibility

Distractibility is linked to attention span, but it also has to do with how perceptive your child is of all that's going on around him. A highly distractible child often seems to wander from activity to activity. These children find it tough to concentrate on a project when they're in a noisy or highly visual environment. This may not be obvious to you at first. It simply seems as if she's constantly jumping down from her seat to wander around, although she does show strong interest in your activity and keeps returning. She may not be able to verbalize or even recall what it was that distracted her in the first place.

With a distractible child, it's especially important to limit the number of choices of activities and to limit the surrounding chaos, as pointed out by Mary Sheedy Kurcinka in the book *Raising Your Spirited Child*.[14] A child who loves to color and also loves to listen to music may not be able to tolerate listening and coloring at the same time because she can't resist the urge to jump up and dance.

At age four, my Aimee was once coloring a picture of the ocean, and I casually said, "Hey, maybe we could go swimming sometime!" She disappeared. I found her in her bedroom, trying on her bathing suit.

Beware of overwhelming your child with too many materials or too many directions at once. Children don't always have the same craving for variety that adults do. It's important to remember how many simple things are still new and interesting to them. To help a child with a short attention span and high distractibility, it helps to start simply. Add new and interesting tools or ideas as your playtime progresses. Instead of handing a toddler a million colors of Play-Doh (or so it seems to him), start with one. When he tires of squishing that, hand him a plastic knife or a single stamping tool. Add a second color or tool later.

As for taking a distractible child somewhere—say, a concert or library story hour, where you'd hate to leave midpoint—you must weigh the benefits versus the potential difficulty with the wiggles. Be sure your expectations of your child are realistic. So you want to expose her to the arts early on. Would she have more fun dancing to classical music on the stereo at home with a sitter while you take the other kids to the symphony? It's not always that black and white; you may opt to take her but plan an early break for her, or take two cars so she can attend half the performance with one parent.

The key here is attitude. You can spend your time feeling frustrated that your child won't pay attention or sit still, or you can accept him the way he is and plan ahead. It may take more planning, but a distractible child still enjoys going places. My wiggly daughter attended a children's concert at age two then talked for months afterward about it, saying, "I wike dose yo-ho-ho songs, in the big tsurts!" (The orchestra played themes from Snow White, and since we had dressed up for the event, she'd assumed the concert hall was a church!)

As for completing activities at home with a distractible child . . . do they *really* have to be finished? Who says? Is it worth the fight? Often the process itself is more valuable than ending a game or finishing a project. The most valuable part of your time together may simply be the way in which you interact and enjoy each other.

As you understand your child's developmental abilities, see resulting milestones she reaches, and learn to teach small measurable skills, you will find it more acceptable to stop activities midway. You can also encourage persistence by thinking, creatively, of ways to continue the activity while altering it slightly.

Do you ever feel too distracted to focus on your child and the activity you are supposedly doing together, as I did in the invisible cookie story? (See chapter 1.) If your child asks for a rolling pin for a project, do you find yourself "just picking up a little" in the kitchen?

It can be really difficult to sit down and roll little snakes out of pink dough when you have a long to-do list. One way to overcome this is to pay close attention to how your child is learning and expressing herself. There certainly will be times when your child can do an activity like this independently. Just be sure you save some time for activities that involve you, too.

Distractibility—what's good about it? With a distractible toddler, you can easily swap your favorite glass figurine with a nonbreakable plastic toy—instead of having to wrench it from a vise grip. At the drop of a hat, you can persuade a distractible preschooler to leap in the car to run errands. This will translate later into a very fun, spontaneous child who will go shopping with you at the last minute!

A child like this tends to get along more easily with others, being less competitive, less involved in games, and more flexible. It's easier to persuade a distractible child to switch tracks when you're bored with a table game. He or she is less likely to care about winning, losing, or finishing and may be willing to try something else you both enjoy.

SENSORY THRESHOLD

A highly distractible child may also be more sensitive to noises, other people's movements, textures, odors, and temperatures. Any or all may distract him from the activity at hand because they are magnified to him. These sensations might be pleasant, unpleasant, or neutral—yet they are distracting nonetheless.

In a school environment, a child may actually fail tests because he's continually distracted. A pencil dropping, a door closing, another child jiggling his leg—all may be ignored by other kids, but not a sensitive one. These are things other children learn to screen out. A child who is easily distracted may be more likely to notice such things, but if he is also very sensitive, noises may actually sound louder to him than to anyone else.

Being accepting of strong sensitivity, and protecting your child from overstimulation when possible, helps. If your daughter insists something bothers her, believe her—no matter how ridiculous it sounds to you. If a child's socks "hurt" because the seam is in the wrong place, try to get her comfortable before attempting to do something fun together. To her the discomfort is very real.

Many children eventually grow out of or adapt to high sensitivity. The same child who screamed bloody murder at age five when her socks hurt may grow into a nine-year-old who calmly cuts the tags out of the neckline of her new clothes. And then you have the adult who stands some days in her closet full of clothes, feeling she has *nothing* to wear. Why? Because she has to find something *soft*. Hmm. I wonder . . . did my socks hurt when I was a child?

ACTIVITY LEVEL

High Activity Level

A high activity level refers to how much and how often a child is moving. A child with "lots of energy" can be a lot of fun . . . or exhausting, depending on your own energy level!

While playing, a high-energy child tends to become rambunctious and rough. That can sometimes get out of control, leading to biting or other unacceptable behaviors. A parent who loves to wrestle needs to look for signs that indicate a child is getting too wound up. It is best not to wrestle immediately before trying to put a high-energy child calmly to bed. (*Hey,* all you daddies out there!)

Some high-energy children can be identified as such in utero. Mama's pregnant belly constantly stretches, jumps, and rolls. Surprise, surprise: After birth, the new baby doesn't seem to require as much sleep as Brother did! Before she can crawl, you feel the energy vibrating in her arms and legs . . . and by ten months, she takes off running. Whew. I've had one, and I can spot one in the arms of another parent a block away.

Some children aren't necessarily excitable but love more physical activities. They may not be overly energetic, but they are drawn to physical activities. Aimee was the busy one in my belly, but Elisa is the one obsessed with mastering her body. This is great if you're physically active yourself. You may enjoy playing tag, a game of basketball, and wrestling on the carpet. But what if you prefer reading stories in the recliner? You may find yourself physically exhausted by an energetic youngster or one who loves sports. Your own energy level is also affected by your current health (which may include pregnancy) and the time of day. If you have had to work all day, you may be exhausted when your child is just getting revved up.

Your child may sit for a story, but unless you actively involve him, he'll be popping up and down like popcorn the whole time. If you have a fun, sedentary activity you'd like to do with your child, you'll be more successful if you help him get his energy out first.

This will probably require some creative thinking. I used to trade child care with another self-employed mom one day a week. To wear out two three-year-olds, I experimented with games that exhausted *them* but not *me*. (I wanted to work on the computer while they napped.) For instance, I would pretend I was a matador, and my "little bulls" took turns charging through a scarf I held out away from me. All I had to do was stand there. Another option is to have a lunch date at a fast-food place with an indoor playground. You can time your child's runs through the mazes and tunnels, cheering him on. Children who simply want to move their bodies (like my Elisa) need regularly scheduled trips to outside playgrounds and times where you move the furniture and roll out pads on which they can do somersaults.

Low Activity Level

What if you have a *low*-energy child? I suspect that this is less frequently a problem, yet if you have a lot of unspent energy or a long to-do list, it can be tough to sit still for a slow-moving child. Even a normally energetic child may run on only two speeds—

SLOW and SLOWER—when Mom or Dad needs to get somewhere fast. Some of this can be associated with distractibility. But it is also apparent that children often resist being hurried!

MOOD AND INTENSITY OF RESPONSES

When playing with our kids, we tend to assume that if we've chosen the right activity, they'll be happy and enthusiastic. But we each have an inborn tendency to be pessimistic or optimistic, sunny or serious. It is important when you play together to consider your child's mood in general. If he's generally pessimistic, try not to take it personally when he complains or analyzes things to death. Of course you can encourage him to lighten up, and it might even work.

A happy-go-lucky child will make you feel like everything you do together is fun and that you are hilarious. A serious child can make you feel like a dud. But it's important to be aware of your child's intensity as well as his general mood. Two children may be extremely pleased with a game you are playing or an outing to the zoo. One of them shows this by smiling slightly, while the other, more dramatic child bursts with enthusiasm, hugs, and kisses. An intense child will let you know—bad or good—how she feels. A less intense child often leaves you wondering how she really feels.

Out of the blue one day, three-year-old Elisa said, " 'Et's go on a baby choochoo train again! Dat one wiff da animals!"

During the train ride at the zoo months before, she had been *completely* silent, apparently drinking in the wonder of it all. We were unaware of how much she had enjoyed it.

Children also express frustration and anxiety in different ways. It's important not to deny or minimize their feelings—even when they are *oh-so-dramatic*. It takes practice to suppress the impulse to eye-roll and say, "Hey! Get over it!" Some children simply slam doors and refuse to speak.

Although you might not expect this to enter into playtimes with you, it no doubt will. Parents do really dumb things, you know. Like cutting a piece of paper in fourths instead of halves when a child innocently asks, "Can you cut this, Mommy?" Then the child sobs, "Nooooo! Not like that! Put it back together!" This is a problem that has faced generation upon generation of parents. Gordy's mother, Ninette, says she *still* recalls a day when her son as a little tyke became hysterical when his hot-dog bun fell apart. "Put it back together!" he had cried.

If only mommies and daddies could patch everything up magically.

APPROACH OR WITHDRAWAL AND ADAPTABILITY

Many children are wary of new situations and people, and some even pull back from new toys or fun activities. Is your child people oriented or more of a loner? gregarious or shy and clingy? affectionate or distant?

If your child is hesitant, it can be a struggle if you're more social and find it easy to jump into new situations. On the other hand, as your child grows up, his hesitancy could very well save him from the problems faced by his more impulsive peers.

This trait is important to be aware of, although it's not likely to present a problem when just you and he play together. It may become an issue, however, if he has difficulty playing independently or seems unable to play with other children.

If you have a child who is slow to warm up to others, and you are gregarious, it may cause you to feel impatient at times. Try to accept your child for who he is, and allow him that time and space to adapt to new situations and friendships.

If your child is stuck to you like glue and you need some space sometimes, it may take extra effort on your part to help your child nurture friendships with other children by arranging play dates. But it can be well worth the effort. You want your child to feel close to you, yet you want him to be able to reach out to peers as well. Your child may not have dozens of friends, but the few he draws close to may be his friends for a lifetime.

REGULARITY

Some kids are quite dependent on regular schedules (sleeping, eating, and toileting), and any disruption of routine can throw them for a loop. If you have a small child who is sensitive to this, you must keep that in mind when planning play activities together. Time may certainly be of the essence. When he gets cranky in the midst of play, think about whether it could be related to his being thrown off schedule. Then consider a new strategy next time around. Once naps are outgrown, you'll have more flexibility, which will make life easier for you both.

MEMORY-GAME POSTSCRIPT

One day shortly before Thanksgiving, Tyler and Aimee received a card from Grandma. The card was a Thanksgiving scene and included stickers of food that the kids could place on it. *Oh, boy,* I thought. *A battle in the making!* Sharing wouldn't be the problem. But I knew Tyler would want the food stickers perfectly organized on the table, while Aimee would happily stick a pumpkin pie in a tree. Tyler's sense of order would not tolerate it.

I decided to cut the sheet of stickers in half and let Aimee stick hers on the card before Tyler knew it existed. (Yup, she happily stuck the turkey sticker under the table in the picture.) If Tyler had had his turn first, he'd have hollered that she "wrecked" the card. This way he had no choice but to cope with imperfection from the start. It worked. A bonus was that I realized later that the stickers were restickable. Tyler got to rearrange them all in his own orderly fashion later. Both kids were happy. I knew that for once I'd made a good decision, based on my understanding of their personality differences.

Understanding your children's temperaments, as well as your own (which may conflict), can make the difference between a fun playtime and a frustrating one. The more you can adapt your activities and expectations to your children's unique traits, the more you will enjoy your kids.

JOKE TIME
Teach your child a new joke or an old one. My son's favorite at age three was:

> *"Why couldn't Cinderella play baseball?"*
> *"She kept running away from the ball!"*

Or how about this knock-knock joke?

> *"Knock knock."*
> *"Who's there?"*
> *"Olive."*
> *"Olive who?"*
> *"Olive you!"*
> *(A hug and kiss go with this one.)*

TELL ME A STORY
Take an old favorite story and have your child tell it to you. You can even close your eyes—but don't fall asleep! Look out for surprise endings. One of my preschoolers had the three bears send Goldilocks to her room for throwing a tantrum. Another had a policeman arrest her for breaking, entering, and porridge theft.

You can also try showing your child paintings of people—for instance, those by Norman Rockwell, which represent a detailed slice of life—and asking your child to make up a story to go with the picture.

i don't feel like playing

Finding More Enthusiasm and Joy in Play

Sigh. You understand the benefits of play, you have time and energy for it, and you understand your children's quirks and abilities. But you just don't feel like playing! Why is it so difficult? You aren't the only parent who lacks joy in play, but guess what? Joy can be found!

"When my son was kindergarten age, a favorite pastime of his was playing with action figures," says Andrea Jones, who currently works as an assistant preschool teacher.

Her son's sentences during play often started with words much like those that little girls use when engaged in doll play: "Pretend this guy does this . . ."

However, unlike Barbie tea parties, Andrea's son's "dolls" focused more on action—particularly the destruction of bad guys. That meant a lot of mock fighting: bumping the figures together while making contact noises, like "Bang!" "Swoosh!" and "Kabam!" This was an activity Andrea's son expected his mom to do as well.

"Now, this can become dreadfully boring pretty quick," says Andrea.

I could certainly relate to the issue of boredom—not necessarily with action figures but with stories I was expected to read or tell over and over. The only thing that made reading about Snow White and her gang over and over and over again tolerable was the funny twist Aimee put on the Seven "Dorfs'" names: Doc, Sleepy, Happy, Stupid, Mad, Sad, and Bafshul.

So far in this book, we've discussed a number of barriers to play—barriers caused by time and energy, barriers that occur when parents don't understand the value of play, and barriers that arise from developmental and personality differences between children. But for many parents, time plus understanding still does not equal enthusiasm.

Lack of motivation to play may come from several arenas:

- Boredom with child play
- Sibling fighting
- Lack of joy with life in general
- Discomfort with play

Andrea is one of many parents who have struggled with boredom during parent-child play. I think you'll be inspired when you read her solution.

BOREDOM BUSTER

To help overcome action-figure boredom, Andrea had to get creative.

"What I began doing was adding humor to the bad-guy scenario—making up stories as we played so that the bad guy would do incredibly stupid, silly things. Of course, I would sneak in as many life lessons as possible. This time turned into a great giggle for both of us and at the same time I was sharing something he chose to play."

One of Andrea's stories included a bad guy robbing a candy store. During his robbery, he's racing around so fast that he bumps into everything. Bumping into things is a natural giggle inducer with young kids. In a great hurry he then tries to carry way too much candy and, of course, drops everything. Since he doesn't want to get caught with the candy, he tries to gobble it all up too fast. He ends up with a stomachache.

As he played, Andrea's son was learning a number of life lessons along the way: Don't steal, Haste makes waste, and the always-important Eating too much candy gives you a stomachache. Even Andrea learned a lesson in this game: There's nothing better than a good giggle!

To prevent feeling antsy during child play, you sometimes need to be proactive as well as creative. Take a little time to find some of the best play materials you can—toys that stimulate the most creative play and offer a variety of ways to play, like a child-sized kitchen. (See chapter 11 for more suggestions on choosing the best toys.) Finding great books to read also helps. If you have a decent selection to choose from, you'll be able to keep your own interest up. Even though kids tend to get locked into favorites, you can usually entice your child into letting you read books you enjoy too.

An awful lot of children's books are dull to read once, let alone over and over again. Unfortunately, these are often the books your children will grab at random from the library shelves because some color on the cover catches their eye. The best way to prevent this is to keep a file folder handy into which you can throw book reviews, book-club book descriptions your kids bring home from school, and a list of appealing titles you've seen in bookstores. When you have a free moment—perhaps while kids nap or have gone to bed—go on-line to your library's Web site and order them. (You can call the library if you don't have a computer.) Within days you will find them waiting for you at the front desk at the library, or if you live in a rural area they may be mailed directly to you. You can rent videos and music CDs this way, too; Elisa and I once rented a hip-hop exercise tape we danced to together.

Keep on the lookout for creative books to buy, borrow, or beg for! And keep in mind that adapting toys in creative ways, as Andrea did, can help deter boredom.

SIBLING SQUABBLING

Many parents report feeling so frustrated with sibling fighting that they have no desire for play. There's something about kids fighting that really puts nerves on edge and makes a mom or dad want to simply leave the room, not play! The racket itself is annoying, but kid fights also create feelings of confusion and helplessness in parents.

One child screams in frustration, "Stupid! I hate you!" while the other teases unmercifully. A sister or brother is impatient with a sibling's undeveloped skills or becomes too competitive and says hurtful things, causing tears. My husband and I get *extremely* annoyed, even angry, in situations like this and tend to do just the wrong thing to try to make things all better, or we do just the right thing—then wonder what it was. "No name calling allowed! No saying that you hate each other! No, no, no!" sometimes works, sometimes doesn't.

My story about the Memory game is a pertinent example of how play between siblings does not always run smoothly. Sometimes it seems a whole day's worth of energy can go into breaking up squabbles or trying to meet the individual needs of more than one child. And when parents play too, it can be a real struggle to meet the needs of everyone involved.

Sometimes one child is especially needy: a baby, an ill or disabled child, or a child with chronic behavioral problems. These require a parent to spend a disproportional amount of time with one kid in particular and can cause siblings to act out in hopes of getting more attention.

Problems are magnified when one child has a personality conflict with a parent, or when Mom or Dad withdraws or becomes angry more often at a child who behaves badly. Contrast that with a sibling who is more pleasant, whom the parent feels more naturally attracted to. No matter how hard a parent tries, that favoritism will show through, which is likely to make the struggling child even more angry and disagreeable.

If an unhealthy cycle is developing, it can lead to the less-favored child fighting more with the favored one. The favored child may even provoke that, knowing Mom or Dad may more easily take his side. These are heavy issues that may need resolving with some professional counseling.

But in the average home, where fighting is simply a way of working out living together with different personalities and needs, there are some good strategies you can try. In *Siblings Without Rivalry*,[15] Adele Faber and Elaine Mazlish state that one common reason kids fight is that they insist on everything being equal, which they equate with fairness. But Faber and Mazlish suggest that instead of worrying about making sure kids are treated equally, it's best to try to focus on what each actually needs.

I think that big kids can understand that a new baby takes an inordinate amount of time. Instead of trying to compensate hour for hour, look for times when your big child feels most needy and set aside time for that. It helps to let the neglected child know you understand. Sometimes just knowing that you long to spend time with him helps.

Kids often ask whom Mom and Dad love most. Isn't first place best? Tell kids you love them for who they are. Your awareness of their personality differences helps, because it can give you specific words to tell them what you appreciate about them.

When kids fight, you may wonder when to intervene and when to keep your distance. It can be hard to let kids work things out between themselves, especially when you are sitting between them! If you can't smooth things over easily or distract the kids from their argument, it's reasonable to say, "I can't sit here and play with you two while you fight. Can you find some way to patch things up so we can get on with our game?"

Sometimes kids can be quite creative about making up when the carrot is more time with Mom or Dad. However, keep in mind that the kind of activity you choose—after considering your children's ages, interests, and personalities—will help prevent many fights from occurring in the first place.

WHERE'S THE JOY?

At some point, nearly all parents experience boredom with children's repetitive activities, and most parents admit to feeling frustration with sibling fights. But for some, the lack of desire when it comes to play runs much deeper. You may love your children dearly yet feel very awkward about play in general, especially spontaneous play.

Part of this might be attributed to your basic personality. Introverts find that being with other people is tiring, and they need to recharge by spending some time alone. Extroverts, on the other hand, are charged up by contact with others, and they tend to be more expressive and perhaps spontaneous. If you have an introverted personality, you may not be inclined to be very emotionally expressive in play, and childish chatter and energy may wear you out. However, I hope that you don't use personality typing to avoid trying things a little out of your comfort zone. Trying these things may help you develop a more warm, playful relationship with your children.

For example, some parents lack enthusiasm for play because they feel little purpose and sense of accomplishment in the day-to-day work of parenting. If you used to work outside of the home but have now chosen to stay home full-time with little ones, you may miss the concrete feedback and encouragement you got from adult coworkers (or even that paycheck, which somehow declared that what you were doing was worth something). Scraping dried Cream of Wheat cereal off linoleum is bound to be less inspiring than clinching a great financial deal for a client. However, I hope that as you read through this book you will gain a sense of the value of parenting and of your capacity to have a tremendous impact on your children's lives—even if no one has handed you a parent trophy yet.

One advantage to being home all day with kids is that, while there is some grunt work involved in child care, you have the luxury of a little time left over to simply hang with your kids. I truly believe that this is one reward for all the work involved in parenting, a "paycheck," so to speak. Even working at home can become so frenzied that intimacy with children begins to slip away. When this happens to me, I have to remind myself to slow down and take time to reap the rewards of being a parent— rewards to myself as well as to my children.

Besides personality differences and a general sense of purpose (or lack thereof), your level of enthusiasm for play can be affected by depression. Sometimes depression or fear of criticism stems from having grown up in an abusive or neglectful home. If you lacked a connection with healthy, playful adults when you were a child yourself and had few role models for parent-child play, then it's likely that your past will affect how playful you feel with your own children.

I DON'T KNOW HOW TO PLAY

Carol wept. "I've always thought that something was very wrong with me, because I don't enjoy playing with my own kids. I fear they sense that and have already been damaged." With her tears flowed thoughts and feelings she had held in since her children—now a preteen and teen—were babies. "I am envious of other mothers who enjoy playing with their babies and children and enjoy being with them." Carol has felt so isolated, believing that few other parents experience such lack of joy in parent-child play.

But Carol is not an uninvolved, uncaring mother. Her closest friends, many of whom have known her for decades, see her as a very normal, loving parent. She has even been a role model for other parents and has led a mother's group to encourage others to pray for their children and their children's teachers. She and her husband take the kids on family vacations, and she has always supported her kids' interests, inside and outside of school. She is compassionate and supportive of others.

Perhaps that's made it too easy for Carol to hide her struggles with play. Because her two children are quite well adjusted, there has been no reason for anyone to see her as a parent needing parenting support. And because of a general lack of openness among parents about common play struggles, Carol has felt quite sure she must be unlike most other parents. She says she can't recall ever feeling playful, although friends have seen her family doing many playful things.

Carol's ongoing struggle with low-grade, yet persistent, depression no doubt colors her perception of *never* having pleasure in play with her children. When someone is depressed, it's difficult to recall good times. But Carol's feelings of numbness and sadness can be traced all the way back to her own childhood, when joyful, healthy play was experienced only occasionally with her parents. As a child she was often expected to be a confidant for her emotionally needy mother, and Carol often avoided her distant and sometimes raging father. Carol was also expected to be a "little mother" to the numerous foster children who were present when she was growing up.

A child needs to be a child and to have a parent to look to for guidance, example, and support. Healthy play often includes role playing—you pretending to be the child and your child pretending to be the grown-up—but true role reversal should never be part of the parent-child relationship. Carol's mother inappropriately told her child things which would have been more appropriate to share with an adult friend. She was emotionally dependent on Carol— quite a burden for a child.

How can a parent inherently know how to play with her children if playfulness was never even a part of her own childhood? Certainly Carol isn't the only one who struggles with play. There are many parents who are walking wounded, having grown up experiencing:

- ◎ An overly rigid home, where play was discouraged and discipline prized
- ◎ Emotional or physical abuse from parents or siblings
- ◎ Childhood trauma outside of the home, including abuse from outsiders
- ◎ Mental illness or substance abuse in parents, causing parental neglect and possibly role reversal in children (the child helping care for the dysfunctional parent)

In *Healing the Scars of Emotional Abuse,* Gregory L. Jantz, Ph.D., states that not only does emotional abuse "damage a person's self-esteem at the time, it also sets up a life pattern that daily assaults the inner being." He adds that relationships are filtered through the negative messages.[16]

If as a child you were continually screamed at, put down, ignored, or expected to fill adult roles, that qualified as emotional abuse. If you are continuing similar patterns with your own children, it's critical to get to the root of those hurts so that they do not get passed on to the next generation.

Dr. Jantz states that common long-term effects of emotional abuse include low self-esteem and lack of self-confidence, perfectionism, inappropriate relationships, unrealistic guilt, and unresolved anger and resentments. All of these are bound to affect parent-child play in some way. How could they not?

If you grew up with a great deal of unpredictability—a Jekyll and Hyde personality in a parent—that could easily make you uncomfortable with lack of control or structure. And kids, by nature, are unpredictable! If you grew up repeatedly hearing emotionally abusive statements, how do you replace those scripts in your mind when your own children make you angry? If you did not feel unconditional love or appropriate physical affection as a child, how do you express it to your own children? Add to all that your unfamiliarity with play and guilt about taking time for play.

Even if your parents weren't necessarily abusive but simply absent, you still might respond in several different ways. Not wanting to repeat the cycle, and desiring to give your kids what you did not receive, you may make special efforts to be involved with your children and to play with them. You may even spend more time with your children than other parents you compare yourself to, but due to low self-esteem, you can't recognize that. And you sense for some reason that quantity time has not been the quality time you'd like it to be. You may even approach play as a duty and an obligation to your child, instead of seeing it as a gift to you both.

You may fear not being involved enough or good enough, knowing how much it hurt you not to have your own parents involved in your life. You may even be playful enough on the surface that your children aren't aware of your lack of enthusiasm or discomfort with child play.

Or you may do the opposite, avoiding involvement with your children because you don't know how to interact in fun and healthy ways. You might even figure that since you turned out okay, your children really don't need you to play with them as long as they have friends or siblings. I hope in this book I am able to persuade you that the way you play with your kids is different from, and in many ways more nurturing than, the way kids play together.

Dealing with childhood trauma can require a lot of work, but it brings the hope of unlocking feelings of playfulness. And that "work" (perhaps with a counselor) can be very worthwhile if it ultimately makes you more optimistic about the future. It will also take practice to learn how to play and to become more spontaneous, but that, too, is possible and worthwhile. Why? As you learn to relax with and enjoy your children, you will draw closer to them and ultimately experience more joy in parenting.

SOLUTIONS

To help release more playfulness within yourself, try the following:

Acknowledge Your Struggles to Others

If you struggle with play in general, it's important for you to recognize that you aren't alone in your feelings; other parents have felt as you do. You may realize that the way you were raised affects your feelings of playfulness. If you're willing to share your feelings about play with other parents whom you see as more playful than yourself, you may find that they are willing to share ideas with you and even show you how to play.

One mom in our neighborhood was known to her neighbors as a mother who played. It was obvious that she was teaching her child a lot through play and enjoying parenting. When a few neighbors asked her *how* she did that, this mom invited them to her home, encouraged them to get down on the floor with her and the kids, then showed the other mothers how to play pretend games using little Fisher-Price people.

I'd love to see more moms mentoring moms (or dads mentoring dads) in the area of play. Wouldn't it be great if, just as La Leche League volunteers mentor mothers who find breast-feeding a challenge, parents could help other parents learn how to play? If more parents who struggle are willing to ask, those who enjoy play would probably be delighted to offer help. Let's look at some other ways you might nurture new feelings of playfulness. For starters, how about thinking of it as a "skill" you can learn, practice, and ultimately enjoy?

Learn the Skill of Playfulness

Feeling comfortable about who you are—extrovert or introvert— is important, but I hope you don't identify so closely with your personality type that it becomes an excuse for feeling a lack of playfulness. How you express yourself and the ways in which you play (remember the variety in chapter 1?) are unique to you. Not everyone has to be a stand-up comic. But all parents should be sensitive to the funny things in life that can draw out a spirit of playfulness.

Do preconceived ideas about how people will think or feel about you, or fears that they may judge you, stifle your ability to play? Do you fear derisive laughter or loss of respect? Well, think about this: Is that the way you feel about others when you see them playing with their kids, no matter how silly they are? Do you lose respect for them, or do you gain it?

Experimenting with new ways to be playful may feel very awkward. Play therapist Mike Weiford believes learning how to play is a bit like learning how to play an instrument or ride a bike: It's never easy at first. But he believes that with practice, play can become more natural and eventually a skill that won't be forgotten.

With some serious and more introspective children, a general sense of humor and spontaneous playfulness must be nurtured. If such a child has been born into a nonplayful family—or, worse yet, has been born into an abusive one—she may easily have her feelings of playfulness squelched.

Tyler, from babyhood on, would do anything to get a laugh, even risking looking silly or clumsy. Aimee was always easygoing and smiling. Elisa is a true delight to us, yet she is far more cautious in her attempts at humor. She has always been more inclined to worry that when people laugh, they're not laughing at her jokes but at *her*. If she remotely suspects the latter, she becomes angry and reclusive. On more than one occasion in her preschool years, she mystified visiting adults who laughed joyfully, not mean-spiritedly, at how cute she was by taking off for her room, upset.

And yet Elisa has the capacity to be very funny—to provoke laughter deliberately. Her sense of humor is being cultivated as she observes it in others, yet she always adds her own personal twist. Elisa cleverly lifts lines from funny movies—lines she knows already generate laughter so perhaps they seem less risky—and plops them into everyday conversations. At age three she would burst into the living room and say in a deep voice, "Hi, honey, I'm home!" which slayed the grandparents. (Incidentally, I can't think up much original material for jokes, but I'm great at stealing material from my kids—thus fooling people into thinking *I'm* the funny one!)

Elisa obviously appreciates playfulness in the rest of her family. In the car one day, completely out of the blue and quite seriously, she said, "We should be called the silly family, because we are so funny."

I asked, "Is that a good thing?"

She responded. "Yeah, 'cause we all like to make people laugh—Daddy, you, Tyler, Aimee, and me."

Yes, laughter is a good thing. But sensitivity is as well. I'm so glad we have Elisa in our lives not only to remind us of how different personalities can learn playfulness but to help keep us sensitive to the feelings of others. And I strongly suspect that the ways I've seen her learn and practice playfulness are ways that adults can learn and practice as well.

Learn to Laugh

How can you introduce more humor into your life? An interesting phenomenon is the emergence of laughter clubs across the country. People go to these groups and literally laugh at nothing in particular, except the sound of their own laughter. They practice saying, "Ho, ho," and "Ha, ha," until they begin to laugh at how silly they sound. This eventually leads to a round of real laughter. Why do they do this? Because the simple act of laughing exercises various muscles and releases healthy chemicals into the bloodstream. They claim that the body responds in a healthy way to laughter whether the cause is real or imagined!

But frankly, I think it's not so hard to seek and find the real McCoy—truly joyful, split-a-gut laughter—when children are in our lives. I couldn't resist telling one laughing group a funny anecdote about Tyler to inject some real-life humor into the session.

Yet in addition to experiencing joy with my children, I admit that I do experience joy in my personal faith in God as well, so the line gets a bit muddied for me. Perhaps I experience joy with my kids because I see them as created beings, uniquely designed, with a purpose in life. I see my relationship with my children in the same way: it's purposefully designed. I think when a parent truly recognizes how unique and valuable he or she is (I hope I can persuade you of that in this book), joy will eventually spill out of that.

There can even be joy and laughter in the midst of sorrow, or during healing from otherwise painful events. At the Women of Faith conferences currently held in stadiums across the country, the women who speak offer bits of wisdom, blended with humor, from their painful backgrounds. Some of those speakers are absolutely hilarious. Their books, including _We Brake for Joy,_ are compilations of poignant and funny stories.

In one such story, Marilyn Meberg describes the loving playfulness between herself and her now-deceased husband. They silently but repeatedly took turns taking the sticker from an Ajax can and sticking it inside each other's dress clothing—in irritating, hard-to-reach places—just before the other would have to stand up (wiggling and tugging at . . . what was that?) before a group. They continued the fun until the sticker's stickiness finally wore off.

I couldn't resist reading that to my kids to show them how playfulness can continue on into adult relationships. Days later, after I'd forgotten about having read that, I was talking with a group of people at church when I kept feeling a strange poke in the middle of my back. Aha! There was a sticker in my dress and Elisa was the grinning culprit.

When Marilyn, despite grieving over the loss of her lifetime playmate, shared her little story, little did she know that it would lead to a little inside joke between a mother and her five-year-old daughter.

My Grandma Gladys, in her nineties, had a lot she could have groused about, considering she was legally blind and the rest of her body was not in the best shape either. And yet she always had a *Reader's Digest* joke or a funny story to share with me over the phone. She "read" magazines by listening to them on records for the blind she had obtained from the public library! I doubt you will have to go that far to find a little humor. Look for funny stuff, and it's likely you'll find it—as near as your grocery check-out stand.

Be open to humor, and sometimes it will surprise-attack you. Some rare children's stories are like that. You open them up to read them, mostly to please your child, and you end up laughing yourself. I remember one story that made me laugh so hard that I was gasping and wiping my eyes while my child rolled his eyes impatiently. It was a story about a pig and duck on a vacation that turns to disaster—something any adult traveler can identify with.

When your own kids say something funny, take a moment to process it and think about *why* it was funny. Add it to your family lore. When Tyler was studying Spanish, we often talked about his studies at the dinner table. Once when Elisa asked if she could have candy for desert, I said, "Maybe." She responded with great confidence and a big grin, *"Maybe* means *yes* in Spanish!" The more we thought about that the funnier it was to us, and it's now becoming a catchphrase whenever anyone says, "Maybe."

Kids' bloopers—mispronunciations of words or phrases—can be humor producers as well. Words can even become part of a family's own code language. *Toe-cram* instead of *toe-jam, crunch-ons* instead of *croutons,* and *super-really hugs* instead of ordinary hugs are a few from our household. Create your own family glossary and reflect back on it occasionally. Once in a while, tell someone else about funny stuff your kids say and put a little laughter into her day. It may not only make her laugh but may jog her memory about funny things her own kids have said. Hey, you might even spread the humor to millions by submitting your funny story to a magazine!

Practice Playing

If you are uncomfortable with play, or at least with a particular age group, consider attending a parent-child class or parenting group where you can get tips and modeling from others. These are often sponsored through hospitals, churches, or park districts.

Just remember that other parents in these groups may feel as awkward as you do, and as you learn more about play, you could end up modeling play for someone else! Be honest with the leader of the group about your needs and ask if this is the right group for you.

Play groups will have differing dynamics, so you might need to play the field a little to find one that's right for you. A batch of insecure parents, when lumped together, occasionally end up spending more time comparing their baby's skills than encouraging one another. An effectively run group should not be too chaotic or noisy, and it should be conducive to play modeling or adult conversation. Well-run groups often become so supportive, so tight, that group members end up meeting with each other for years. Several times I've met groups of parents at the park with their preschoolers and come to find out that these parents met in childbirth or early-education classes. Some even ended up creating co-ops to trade child care.

Weiford suggests that another training ground for learning how to play might be the church nursery, where parents less comfortable with play can volunteer to shadow other parents who enjoy it. If you feel uncomfortable with play, especially with a specific age group, you might find out if you can sit in on a class with that age group, to see how the teacher interacts with the kids.

Take a Class

My friend Barbara is, by nature, an introvert. Last year, the thought of getting up in front of a group of people made her uncomfortable. But she has always felt it important to support and encourage her daughters' strengths while also encouraging them to find ways to overcome their weaknesses, so she thought perhaps she should follow her own advice.

Barbara decided to do something out of character for herself—and a little intimidating at first. She began taking some theater classes, because it went against her natural instinct, which was to be in the audience instead of onstage.

The class surprised her. The teacher insisted the students get up and perform spontaneously without fear of criticism. Barbara and her fellow students were praised merely for having the courage to get up in front of the others and try something spontaneous. And as Barbara began to relax, she found it was actually fun. Surprise, surprise, it was also fun to take home some improvisational games she learned, to play with her four-year-old!

Then, within the year, Barbara bravely accepted a position as hospitality chairwoman of a hundred-member writers group. That included—oh, my!—greeting newcomers with a microphone from the front of the room. No one suspects it doesn't feel natural to Barbara. Although she doesn't gain the energy from public speaking that an extrovert might, this small step of boldness has become a tool for her to connect more with other people in the writing industry, which was one of her goals.

In the same way, learning play skills can help meet a goal of spending time with your children. In the process of practicing playfulness as a skill, you will reap great benefits: long-term, intimate relationships with your kids. And I suspect you'll eventually find yourself laughing . . . despite yourself.

Nurture Your Own Playfulness

If it's difficult for you to play without feeling guilty, it may be time for you to take a class or join a group to do something purely fun for yourself, instead of to practice skills you're not yet comfortable with. As you begin to have more fun on your own, your uplifted spirit may be more open to playing with your kids and relaxing with them.

What's your pleasure? book clubs? music? flower design? Try something new, or take time to cultivate your own style at something you know you do well. Give yourself permission to play by yourself, as long as this never completely substitutes for playing with your kids. If you can find a hobby you enjoy and your child enjoys it too, you'll get a double blessing.

Carol, the tormented mom I talked about earlier in this chapter, began taking art classes that tap into her creativity and bring her a sense of enjoyment. She's gained more of a zest for life. When she returns from her classes, her son (who also has artistic tendencies) excitedly asks her, "What did you learn tonight?" She enjoys sharing new skills or techniques with her son, who is now in junior high. This draws them closer to each other. Carol has found, as many parents do, that she has enjoyed her children more since they've reached the upper grades. This should offer hope to parents who struggle with the baby and preschool stages. However, keep in mind that the time and energy you put into your relationships with your kids before they hit their preteen years will pay big dividends to you in the long run.

5 minute fun

BABY BUZZ

Here's one way to get a giggle from a baby. Try this finger play (author appreciated yet unknown):

> *Here are the beehives (make fists)*
> *Where are the bees?*
> *Hidden away, where nobody sees.*
> *Here they come creeping, out of the hives . . .*
> *One, two, three, four, five! (open fingers one by one)*
> *Bzzzzz . . .*

I liked to add "Tickle bees!" at the end when I played this with baby Elisa. Then I would tickle her under her chin. It didn't take long before all I had to do was hold up my fists and say, "Tickle bees!" to get her wriggling and smiling in anticipation! Check your library or bookstore for books with other finger plays.

CELEBRITY INTERVIEW

Deepen your voice and thrust your microphone (your fist) near your child. Ask him, as if you are a news reporter, the following: "Tell me, sir, what is your name? your favorite toy? your favorite food?" You might be surprised at what you discover. You might even use a real microphone and play back the tape so he can hear himself.

AMATEUR MUSICIANS

Keep a tambourine, maracas, xylophone, and bells in a box near the stereo. Or set out a few props for your kid to use to play pretend: a tennis racket makes a good guitar, a toilet paper roll makes a great microphone, and an empty oatmeal container makes a dandy drum!

The Effect of Family Stress on Play

Is there something in your life that seems to get in the way of everything, including play? Is your stress something difficult, yet quickly passing? Or has it interfered with play longer than you can remember?

I lay on the couch, hunched into a ball, hands on my nauseated stomach. It was "only" the flu, but I felt awful. Even worse, I simply could not keep up with sixteen-month-old Tyler. I watched helplessly as he found a few pennies on the floor and tried to eat them. Then he climbed perilously to the top of the dining-room table. All I could do was lie there and weakly whisper, "No, no!"

When he wasn't racing around, he was crawling all over me. That kept him safer, but my body ached. I yearned to be left alone so I could crawl into bed.

Fortunately, when Gordy came home, I was able to escape to bed without worrying about Tyler. However, the next morning, when I awoke to the baby's crying, Gordy had already left for work, and I still felt horrible. All I could do was pray, *Lord, I just can't make it today without you. You will have to take charge of my home today. Please help me, and keep Tyler safe!*

After Tyler and I had been up for a few hours, I felt a bit better. It was a beautiful, sunny day and my son begged to go "Owside! Owside!" I finally relented and put him in his stroller, hoping the fresh air would revive me.

We headed up the hill, but after a few blocks I turned

around, lacking the energy to go farther. I must have been a pitiful sight—shuffling home one inch at a time, crouched over the stroller as it supported my weight. On our way past my neighbor's house, she cracked open her door and leaned out.

"Are you all right? You don't look well."

Feeling dizzy, I gave Helen a weak smile. I replied, "Oh, it's just a flu bug. I thought I was getting over it, but I'll be okay. Thanks for asking."

"I've heard that flu is going around—hope you feel better soon."

As the stroller bumped and jerked on our gravel driveway, I steadied it with one hand and felt my forehead with the back of the other. Hot. My brain felt foggy. Thank goodness, we were home.

I lugged Tyler—who seemed twenty pounds heavier—up the stairs and in the door. I collapsed on the couch. I tried to read Tyler a few stories, but my stomach felt so terrible it was hard to concentrate. I resorted to TV, the electronic baby-sitter, hoping that might hold his attention for a while.

I wondered what in the world might make me feel better. No over-the-counter medicines had done the trick. *Hmm. I've heard that peppermint tea soothes the stomach; maybe that will work.*

I knew I didn't have any in the cupboard, so I thought I'd try to drive to the store. But as I grabbed my purse, I realized I felt too ill to drive. Oh, well. Maybe the tea wouldn't help anyway.

As I stood there, halfway to the door, keys in hand, the doorbell rang. Who might that be? I sure wasn't up for entertaining. Hesitantly I opened the door to find Bill, Helen's husband, standing there.

"Helen wanted me to give you this," he said while handing me a small, colorful bag, "since you're not feeling well."

I smiled, then opened the bag. Inside were some balloons, cookies, and—of all things—peppermint tea! I stood staring at it in amazement.

After exclamations, thanks, and good-byes, I put on the tea-kettle and then blew up a few balloons. Tyler was soon occupied and giggling. Within minutes, I was relaxing in the recliner, sipping my tea. To my amazement, it soothed my stomach as nothing else had.

Although I had no strength to play, I could lie on the couch and watch my child. I was grateful that the simple gift of a few balloons allowed us to "play" in the only way I could manage at that moment.

I also felt grateful for the creative way my desperate prayer for help had been answered, through the hands of willing neighbors.

WHEN PLAY FEELS IMPOSSIBLE

The purpose of this chapter may surprise you. It is designed to give you permission *not* to play, or to play in extremely simple ways, without guilt when you're simply not able. It's important that we recognize the impact stress has on play.

When you think of stress, what comes to mind? Life in general? a recent episode of some sort? Stress may be caused by something as minor, yet debilitating, as the flu. Or it may be as devastating as a death in the family. Some stresses we choose, such as moving or having a new baby. Others surprise us, such as sudden unemployment or injury to a family member. Physical stress often prevents us from having time or energy for play. Emotional stress—including anxiety, fear, or depression—can easily prevent us from *enjoying* play.

Advising you to play as usual when you are under stress would be about as effective as sticking a bandage on a broken leg. I'm realistic about my limits here, and addressing any one stress in depth is beyond the scope of this particular book. However, I can offer a few thoughts that might make things just a little bit better for you. Simple play—when that's all you can manage—can help heal your raw emotions; it can even boost your immunity to illness.

Researchers have created a table of stresses, assigning risk points to stressful events based on their impact on the immune system.[17] For instance, death of a spouse scored 100; major injury or illness, 53; and moving, 20. The greater the number of risk points, the more vulnerable you are to bacteria and viruses. Lack of sleep, failure to exercise, and missed meals compound the problem. Resolving the stress in your life will offer you health benefits in addition to helping you enjoy parent-child play more.

Even stresses we *choose* still cause stress. For example, choosing to move to a new state for a new job, when the previous job was secure yet unrewarding, may benefit your family in the long run, but even chosen stress zaps energy levels. Moving requires hundreds of little decisions. It's easy to become irritable, exhausted, and distracted from your kids. Children, noticing that tension, may misbehave in uncharacteristic ways, and this adds yet more tension.

When stressful situations are not chosen and are sudden, a dark cloud of insecurity often compounds stress. Unemployment or other financial worries can also be distressing, even all-consuming.

PHYSICAL STRESS

When our bodies, or the bodies of those we love, don't work right, it's shocking to realize how helpless we really are. We may be disabled with something temporary like the flu, or we may experience a physical stress for years. Some physical stresses come on gradually. Others overwhelm us without warning. Physical stresses include:

- Chronic or frequent pain (back pain, migraines, or joint pain)
- Chronic fatigue syndrome or any long-term illness
- Difficult pregnancy (possibly with bed rest)
- Miscarriage
- Medical crisis in a spouse or child

Cassie had a seemingly ideal parenting situation with her toddler Meg, a precocious and golden-curled Shirley Temple lookalike. They played together so much that Cassie occasionally wondered if she might be making Meg too dependent on her.

Nevertheless, it was thrilling, almost addictive, to see how her daughter's bright little mind soaked up information through play and everyday circumstances. With Meg eagerly leading, Cassie took seriously her new role as mother and teacher and reveled in it.

Then baby Luke burst onto the scene.

Poor Luke. His little stomach ached incessantly from gastric reflux. He cried constantly. All day, day after endless day for nearly a year, he rarely slept for more than two hours at a time—even at night. Cassie recalls, "Sometimes I'd put him down and he'd sleep for twenty to forty minutes, then wake up and cry for two hours straight."

But (as said the cat in *The Cat in the Hat*) that is not all! Oh, no. That is not all.[18]

Cassie also suffered from severe migraines and back pain, the results of a long-ago auto accident, and these were compounded by hours of holding Luke in awkward positions in the middle of the night. Meg, then three and a half, struggled with toilet training and was a terribly picky eater. So, in addition to exhaustion and pain, Cassie had emotional stress—guilt over missing playtime with Meg and worry about her becoming emotionally maladjusted.

Physical stress *absolutely* affects how playful you feel and how much time and energy you have for play. When simply getting through a day seems monumental, playing with your child in addition may seem difficult, if not impossible.

A medical crisis in your extended family can be equally draining. When my own mom had a stroke, I had to quickly jump on a plane with twenty-one-month-old Aimee. The following weeks were a blur of intensive-care visits, medical decisions, agonizing uncertainty about whether my mom would survive, toddler chasing, and attempts to coordinate Gordy's work schedule with sitters for Tyler, who was still back home.

As for play? All I could manage was to buy a doll for Aimee between hospital visits and to tuck my son in at night over the phone. Simply getting through those dark days was enough. If you live closer to injured or ill parents or siblings, you might be involved with long-term care, which becomes more of a long-term stress.

PERMANENT LOSSES

Reminders of permanent losses, especially deaths in the family, may not stress us out all year long, but they resurface rather predictably at certain times of the year—say, around holidays or the birthday of the loved one who is gone. It's important to not shrug off how that affects us, because it certainly affects how playful we feel with our children on those recurring dates.

A few years ago, I was standing in three-year-old Elisa's room, looking in her clothes closet. A wave of extreme sadness washed over me. At first I wondered, *What's wrong with me?* I'd been feeling low all day and had been snapping at the kids.

Then I realized it was the week of my father's birthday and the anniversary of his death from a fatal traffic accident. But that had been thirteen years before! How could it still hurt so much? I touched a tiny OshKosh jumper. My dad had never had the opportunity to meet my lovely children, nor they, he. I think that we need to give ourselves some grace on the anniversary of those painful dates. Anticipating that they might be difficult, and planning something special on those dates, can help. When my best friend, Cyndi, got married, both my girls were in the ceremony with me. In all the excitement I forgot that it was the same week I lost my dad years ago. Of course, I can't make Cyndi remarry Lester every year! But perhaps planning something else to look forward to with the children—some playful, fun event—may help in the future.

PARENTING WITH EXTRA CHALLENGES

Sometimes parenting itself is complicated by such things as:

- Stepparenting
- Adoption or foster parenting
- Parenting a child with serious behavioral problems
- Teen pregnancy or runaway
- Substance abuse or illegal activity on the part of a child
- Marital struggles, possibly including abuse

Some of those complications are chosen willingly, like stepparenting, foster parenting, or adoption. But that doesn't make them any less challenging—especially when they involve assimilating an older child with problems into a new family structure. One family who adopted a five-year-old from Russia discovered that the child had been so emotionally wounded before she came to America that her ability to bond with her new parents and act appropriately with her new siblings was severely impacted. Her new family is dedicated to her, but the child's struggles create stress nonetheless. Handling misbehaviors can steal a lot of time in a day—time that might otherwise be used for play.

Other parenting challenges arise unexpectedly when a child who has formerly been fairly well adjusted goes astray and makes terrible choices. That sometimes happens even when a child is raised in a loving home by parents with older children who made great choices. A child's personality, particularly that of a child with a very strong will and a high level of impulsiveness, may lead him to make mistakes and learn consequences the hard way. In this day and age, we must be open to, even diligent about, discussing drugs, alcohol, and sex with children before they enter their teen years. Yet even frank discussions may not deter a child if he is exposed to unhealthy peers. We must be ever wise and watchful—attitudes which sometimes seem to conflict with playfulness. Anticipating potential problems and figuring out what to do when they arise can be emotionally exhausting.

For many parents, marital struggles are often piled on top of other struggles. "I had everything in life that would appear to make for a happy and contented marriage," says Kelli, mother of two. She had a devoted (yet controlling) husband, a nice home, healthy kids, and few financial concerns. She had never been physically abused, nor had she ever felt the threat of physical abuse.

"But," she said, "the cutting, critical, blaming, and shaming words of my husband were wounding my heart and soul." She felt responsible for his moods and it required significant energy on her part to continually smooth things over. "That obviously left little freedom, safety, or energy for play!"

Long-term stress caused by physical and emotional abuse can become so intricately woven into daily life that it requires a dramatic decision to break free from that stress. Many women endure physical and emotional abuse throughout their children's lives. Daily doses of anxiety and fear interfere with pleasure in parenting as well as enjoyment in life itself. Feeling safe and secure is a basic need that must be met (according to Maslow's hierarchy of basic needs, which I referred to in chapter 3) just after the need for food, air, and water—and before you can focus on intimacy and self-expression. Children in abusive homes often experience anxiety and fear that follow them into their adult and parenting lives; only parents can stop that cycle.

SO WHAT'S A PARENT TO DO?

Solutions to dealing with stress are often complicated and long-term. Yet it is possible to overcome some of the ill effects of stress and grow through stressful experiences. Consider the following steps:

Differentiate between Short- and Long-Term Stresses

Is the stress you're experiencing short-term, even if intense? Or is it dragging on from one month to the next, even through years? Once you identify your stress as a short- or long-term problem, you'll be better able to consider options for dealing with that stress. I'd qualify my mother's medical emergency when Aimee was a toddler as a short-term stress, despite its intensity, although now that my mother is disabled, there are also some feelings of permanent loss. When stress hangs in your home for the long haul, you do need to consider how it's affecting your relationship with your children.

Has your anxiety or depression been a major focus throughout your daughter's or son's childhood? If so, you must consciously seek ways to break that pattern so you can experience more joy as a parent. If your emotional ill health is causing you to miss meeting some of your children's emotional needs, please consider getting outside help. That might mean joining a parent support group like MOPS (Mothers of Preschoolers) or a group focusing specifically on anxiety. Perhaps you should consider professional counseling or a recovery group.

One day in a doctor's office, I saw a little note that stated, "*Now I can play with my kids*" on an advertisement for an antidepressant medication. While I'm not advocating medication as a *universal* treatment for stress—or even for chronic depression—that was the first time I'd ever seen recognition that emotional health affects parent-child play. Depression may prevent you from meeting your children's basic needs for affection and attention, and it may also affect your own physical health.

Long-term stress can also be caused by post-traumatic stress from an event you personally experienced or witnessed, or by abuse you or a child may have experienced or are experiencing.

Think about Your Reactions to Stress

Do you overreact when your children squabble with each other? explode in anger at minor things? forget promises to your children or appointments that are meaningful to them?

Children are smart and sensitive. To some degree, it's important that we be honest with them when we feel stressed, without burdening them with unnecessary details. Acknowledge to your children that you love them. Apologize if you snap at them. Tell them you feel worried or sad and that it will pass. Let them know that they have not done anything wrong, and if you're working on your own emotional issues, tell them that it doesn't have to do with them. Older children will most likely respect you for your honesty and willingness to break a painful or damaging generational cycle or pattern.

Know Your Limits

Any stress, chosen or unchosen, should cause us to pause and think critically of the other ways we are spending our time and energy. Consider which activities you can cut out in order to ease some of the stress in your life.[19] The Cat in the Hat juggled a cup, fish, cake, and more, saying, "Look at me, look at me, look at me now!" Finally his routine fell apart with messy results. That's not unlike the superparent juggling so many tasks—plus stress—that her routine falls apart and her emotions with it.

One symptom I experience when I fall apart is extreme forgetfulness. When I find myself (more often than usual) running downstairs to grab something, then forgetting what I ran to grab, I know my stress is catching up with me. Fewer scheduled commitments often helps, because merely looking at a full calendar when I'm stressed makes me freeze. So, at least until a stressful event passes, instead of signing a kid up for gymnastics lessons—which you must remember every Tuesday at 10:30—let your child use a mat at home.

Simplify your life. Instead of going to that optional PTA meeting, sit and cuddle your child. Have him tell you his own funny version of "The Three Bears." Give your child the limelight, and give yourself a little downtime to relax your body and mind. When you're too tired or sad or in too much pain to think straight, perhaps all you can muster is to stop, watch, and listen to your child. And that may be enough. If you're having trouble keeping on top of your housework in addition to the stress you're experiencing, it's okay to say no to messy modeling clay or table games. Give your child a massage and let her give you one. A five-year-old can give a great shoulder rub!

Cassie, the mom I mentioned earlier in the chapter, worried when Meg was little that watching too much television would harm Meg. Now she says, "If I had to do it all over again, I would have used TV more with Meg during that time with Luke. Kids really can survive television." (Parent-selected programs, of course!)

Let Others Help You

Outside help includes help from your spouse, family support, support from friends, professional counseling, or medical help. It might mean allowing a friend to hold your crying baby so you can spend a few moments with his sister, out of the house, away from the wailing.

Cassie wishes she had taken more people up on this offer earlier on, so she could have spent time with Meg and taken care of herself better. Although Cassie's folks were a great help from the word *go*— especially with Meg—it wasn't until Luke was about seven months old (and still crying) that Cassie sought additional help. She shared with her church her desperate need for help and found Dawn, a heaven-sent professional nanny who came to the house several days a week. Although it stretched the family budget to hire help, Cassie needed time to take care of some of her own needs, including getting therapy for her back and neck. She thinks that if she had taken time to care better for herself earlier on, she might not be enduring as much back pain now. She put her own health on the back burner to care for her children, as so many of us do.

Help from others may come from within your own family. When Gordy and Aimee came in the room the day I was feeling sad about my father, they knew by the look on my face that something was wrong. "What's wrong, Mom?" asked Aimee. Tears came and I said, simply, that I missed my dad. Nine-year-old Aimee wrapped her arms around me tightly. We stood there, silently hugging.

I think there are times when we should allow a child to comfort us. It can be a precious moment. While it's not healthy to make a child feel responsible for making us feel better, we shouldn't shut them out emotionally. We don't want them to wonder, *Why is mom so testy? so distant? Have I done something wrong?*

When Aimee hugged me, it empowered her and comforted me. I think adults often underestimate how compassionate and understanding children can be. Even Cassie's daughter, Meg, understood that her brother was in pain and made efforts to try to make him feel better. This also gave her a little more sense of control in an out-of-control situation.

Take Joy in Your Children

Determine not to let your current stress cause you to miss out on connecting with your child, enjoying his stage of life and the humor it can bring. Don't focus so much on your own stress that you miss poignant or even funny moments.

I recall how, in the midst of my fretting about my mom's health, I saw Aimee reach in a drawer of dishcloths. I thought she might toss them about, but instead, she ran for her new baby doll and fashioned a diaper for it! My baby was diapering her own "baby." I took a moment to write that down, think about it, and appreciate it.

Consider Seeking Specialized Help,
and Try to Remain Hopeful

My friend Barbara had to accept a different kind of help when she discovered that her eldest daughter was abusing alcohol and drugs, and even ran away temporarily. Barbara had to get help from law-enforcement officials and social services to rescue her child.

Barbara's daughter is doing well now—working and taking college classes. In fact, she wants to help prevent other teens from getting sucked into substance abuse. She supported her mom's decision to write about their struggles, and how they overcame them, not only in a newspaper editorial but in an article published in a national magazine.

Incidentally, Barbara found that the playfulness she'd had with her daughter when she was younger eventually helped restore their relationship. Her teen recently reminisced, "Remember those read-and-fold parties we used to have? Mom, you are so clever!" Not long ago, she asked her mom, "Want to go to a movie with me? It starts at nine-thirty."

Barbara's immediate thought was, *Why didn't you ask hours ago?* She was exhausted from working part-time plus caring for her preschooler, and she already had her pj's on.

However, Barbara caught herself just in time, remembering their turbulent times the year before. She writes, "I said, 'Of course!' and quickly changed my clothes. I stepped out into the chilly night with a warm heart, gladly exchanging a little sleep for a date with my daughter. It was time again to *play!*"

Parents can find support through friendships, social-service organizations, and specialized support groups.

Kelli, the woman who was experiencing emotional abuse in her marriage, has found help through individual counseling and a group at her church that tackles domestic-violence issues. She is becoming more aware of what is unhealthy and how to set boundaries.

She is fortunate that her husband is committed and devoted to her and the family. (Quite often in domestic-violence situations, parents have no recourse but to escape their abusive marriages so they and their children can be safe.[20]) When Kelli confronted her husband with the truth about his emotional abuse, he began to realize the damage his words have caused to his wife *and* others. He is seeking support to find ways to control his verbal abuse. Finally, Kelli is beginning to feel more relaxed and playful.

Also through counseling, Carol, the woman who had difficulty enjoying play, has begun to see how depression has interfered with her relationships with her two children from the time they were small. She is beginning to see how trauma from her own childhood has, in part, shaped her into the mother she is now.

Professional counseling can vary from one counselor to another, so it may take some exploring to connect with someone truly helpful. Please don't give up too easily.

Take Time to Process Your Stress

Over thirteen years, I've become less likely to deliberately think about my dad during the time of year that he died, but my internal clock still knows and remembers. Dad is still gone and will miss every developmental stage my children grow and change through. It's okay to grieve.

I've found that it is healthier for me to take a little time around my father's birthday to *deliberately* think about him, describe him to my children—his grandchildren—and look at photos of him. Although my children never met him, he is their grandfather and they deserve to know about him. It helps ease my pain a little, and it also helps the children to treasure the time they have with *their* dad.

If it's your kids who are stressed out or grieving, play can be an incredible healing tool for them. In play, kids have the opportunity to express their feelings, and it's important to listen to them. Sometimes it helps just for you to acknowledge the way they are feeling.

One single parent, Luci, an elementary-school counselor, tells her son "Hans stories." That's not her son's name, but the stories reflect what he's going through or has experienced. Her child loves this third-person approach to exploring his feelings through stories about a fictional child. "Hans was going to go to the dentist for the first time, and he was *really* scared! But when he got there . . ."

Play therapist Mike Weiford, when engaged in play therapy

with a child, sometimes offers her three different-sized bears. He then asks which bear the child would be, and which bears would be other people in her family. Interestingly enough, if a child feels a little out of balance emotionally, she might choose the biggest bear so she can feel more in control. Playing with puppets or dolls is also a useful way for children to express their thoughts and feelings through made-up dialogue.

If you feel out of your league because your child begins expressing some very intense feelings, or if you know that his stress relates to having experienced abuse, a counselor specializing in play therapy may be able to show you how best to help your child.

When you're stressed, reaching out to others does help. Yet it also helps to reach out to the greatest counselor of all: a merciful God who can, in the midst of illness, send peppermint tea, or, in the midst of anxiety, send a calm peace "more wonderful than the human mind can understand" (Philippians 4:7).

5 minute fun

RECLINER RACE

What can you do with a three-year-old who has boundless energy right when you need a break?

My favorite "game" at times like this was to move my favorite chair to the middle of the living room. I'd sit in it, with a cup of coffee in hand, and ask my child, "Can you run a hundred laps around me?"

I'd time her or count laps out loud with her, or simply cheer, "Go! Go! Hurray! Look how *fast* you are!"

I LOVE YOU MORE THAN . . .

Think of anything your child knows you love, and tell him you love him more than that. He is likely to come back right back with his own love declarations for you.

"I love you more than double-chocolate-chip cookies!"

"I love you more than a triple-scoop ice-cream cone with sprinkles!"

"I love you as high as the moon!"

Read the book *Guess How Much I Love You*,[21] a story describing how much Little Nutbrown Hare and Big Nutbrown Hare love each other.

part 3
harnessing
your
resources

chores are done, time for fun!

chapter 10

Nurturing Kids' Self-Reliance and Helpfulness

Ah, the joys of having responsible children . . .

creating more time and energy for family fun!

The door jingled as we entered the small gift shop.

"There they are!" Aimee said. She held up a little stuffed basset hound. "This one is *so* cute!"

"I want one too!" exclaimed Elisa.

I explained to her, for the second time, that Aimee was spending her own, hard-earned allowance. Elisa looked very unhappy.

"But I want one really, really, *really* bad."

"Well, what could you do to earn it?" I asked my three-and-a-half-year-old.

Elisa stood still, thinking. "How 'bout if I do a chore like Aimee and Tyler every day?" She rambled on about how Tyler does the recycling and Aimee sets the table. Then she said, "I could empty the dishwasher every day, not do the knives 'cause they're too sharp, but I could empty the rest."

I told her it would take her four weeks to earn that eight-dollar stuffed dog, but if she did a great job, she could start earning a regular allowance—two dollars a week! Elisa eagerly agreed, then she stepped up to the counter with the cash I loaned her, a big grin on her face.

Back at home, Elisa kept her promise. Two years later she's still faithfully emptying the dishwasher!

RESPONSIBLY FUN

It's possible to live in a playful, loving home where children are highly responsible and respectful. I know. I live in one. Having responsible kids affects playfulness in the home in these ways:

- It frees up time for family play.
- It builds children's self-confidence, especially when their level of responsibility helps make a fun family outing more successful.
- It decreases stress on parents (having to do all and be all). That can help you feel more playful in planning play and going on outings, and it can give you more energy and time for these things.
- It teaches kids that setup and cleanup are part and parcel of making some play activities successful and fun.

Playfulness also affects responsibility. Chores can be made more tolerable when you keep a sense of humor or use some creativity—they can even be used to teach your children new skills.

Perhaps you're wondering if my kids ever complain about doing chores. Certainly! Lately Elisa has had a mysterious ailment that tends to come and go. It comes at chore time and goes at playtime.

INGREDIENTS FOR RAISING RESPONSIBLE KIDS

Have appropriate expectations: Consider personalities and skill levels, but avoid gender bias if possible.
Evaluate your involvement: Think about what you must do, might do, or should not do for your child.
Choose areas of responsibility: Don't expect too much at once.
Keep your child accountable: Set consequences if your kids don't follow through.
Be willing to teach: Modeling skills now will help you reap benefits later.
Avoid perfectionism: Try not to discourage positive efforts, even if they're not perfect.
Model responsible behavior: (Does that include bed making? Oops.)
Discuss responsible and irresponsible behaviors: Talk about the actions of other people, including television personalities, athletes, or musicians.

"My back hurts," she moans the instant the dishwasher needs emptying.

"Oh, what a shame!" we reply. "You'd better get right to bed!"

She moans a little less, and after putting the last spoon in the silverware drawer, she bounds down the stairs four at a time, miraculously healed! Sometimes we have to nag the kids to do their jobs, but that's usually when our routine has not been consistent for a while. For instance, the kids do fine alternating nights doing the dishes until we have a few nights in a row when I don't cook; then comes the great debate about whose turn it is or isn't.

To be honest, I marvel at how cheerfully Elisa has done her chore for so long. What a bargain for two bucks a week! (I guess it's time for a raise or to let her try something different.) However, I think that particular chore has been easy for her to stick with because the whole kitchen-duty train comes to a screeching halt when her part is not done. The guinea pig may squeak all day to be fed. The laundry could lie around in piles until someone actually needed a fresh T-shirt. But the family can't eat if there are no clean dishes in the cupboard to set the table with, nor can they clean up if there's no place for dirty cups to go. Elisa knows we depend on her—that what she does actually matters. She takes tremendous pride in that.

The same goes for Tyler's job. I am terribly spoiled—I admit it. Every Wednesday, while still in my bathrobe, sipping my latte, I

Offer sympathy on occasion: Chores aren't fun for anyone. (I don't like cleaning toilets either—it simply has to be done.)

Allow consequences: Follow through with consequences, or don't always step in to help your kids when they goof.

Balance work and play: Try to incorporate a good amount of both, with some openness to spontaneity and flexibility.

Strive for consistent schedules: This way, chores become habits.

Minimize bailouts. This helps kids to become more self-reliant and less "mom" or "dad" reliant.

Reward responsible behavior: Let your kids know when they're doing great, without overcompensating.

look out the window and see that yes, indeed, the garbage and recycling have been set at the curb. I can count on one hand the number of times I've had to remind Tyler to get the garbage out in four years—that's 208 weeks! On the very few occasions it didn't make it out in time, we got to smell the garbage in the garage all week. Once when we were charged double for the previous week's can, Tyler got to pay for it. We are *so* mean.

It may surprise you that we are as dedicated to being firm with our kids as we are to playing with them. Tyler used to insist that I was the "strictest mom in town," until a friend of his joined us for dinner and lightheartedly insisted that I was in third place. At least two other moms in town are stricter than I am. (But I still have the *gall* to ask my children to tell me exactly where they will be, with whom, and for how long, and I review movies before letting them go.)

Part of being firm involves not just setting rules but asking kids to do for themselves what you might think "good parents" usually do. I rarely pack lunches for my kids or remind them to do homework. You may be horrified that I don't make my kids' lunches. Well, I think it's my job to be sure they get a good lunch. For my kids, that means making sure they have money for hot lunch, or stocking the cupboards with lunch supplies for them to make their own.

It takes a long view toward the future and determination in the midst of whining and gnashing of teeth to help kids learn to be self-reliant. I read a very helpful book, *MegaSkills* (by Dorothy Rich, with an enthusiastic forward by Barbara Bush), when Tyler and Aimee were small. It motivated me to help my children develop initiative, perseverance, common sense, problem-solving skills, and a host of other "MegaSkills" Rich describes. I love how she uses the "never-ending report card" to illustrate the long-term effects of teaching kids such skills. Note these parallels in her chapter on effort:

> *The Grades We Get in School: Alice likes to do a lot and she tries her hand at almost everything. Alice is a doer. She is ready to do the hard work it takes.*

The Grades We Get on the Job: Mrs. Taylor always seeks opportunities to gain new skills and knowledge. She knows that it takes hard work to make the necessary changes.[22]

It's possible that my occupational-therapy perspective has made me more determined than the average parent to teach my kids how to do things for themselves. I still recall when, in my twenties, I did an internship at a hospital. An elderly man who had suffered a stroke became annoyed with me when I asked him to reach for something he wanted me to hand him.

"Your job is to do it for me!" he spat.

"Actually," I corrected him, "my job is to get you to do it yourself, so you can build up your strength and get out of this hospital." He muttered about how, once he got home, his wife would get him anything he wanted.

Over the years I've seen this scenario replayed when preschool friends have visited my children. Since I've always taken a hard-nosed attitude in teaching my children to dress themselves, I'm often shocked when visiting playmates wordlessly shove their shoes or coat in my face and stand there expecting me to dress them. My kids learned early on that I would feign shock when automatically expected to serve them. A well-timed "You want me to do *what?*" is often all it takes for a kid to realize that a task is not necessarily an adult's role. However, when it's a new task, it's important to add, "I'd be happy to show you how. You try doing this part first, okay?"

When kids can do things for themselves, it's amazing how much easier it is to get out of the house to go do something fun! We've made it on the spur of the moment to many concerts, parades, and movies when I've hollered out, "Everyone get ready; we'll meet in the car in five minutes!"

It's possible my first two preschoolers learned some self-reliance out of necessity. Tyler was three years old when I had morning sickness from my pregnancy with Aimee, and Aimee was in preschool when I had an even more difficult pregnancy with Elisa. (I lost some use of one arm for nine months due to pinched nerves.) Both kids were expected to do anything they could to help themselves, and I must admit I was astonished to discover how capable they could be: dressing themselves, getting their own preschool supplies together, even making their own sandwiches!

They continue to be tremendously faithful with all school-related responsibilities. I can't recall the last time I woke a child up to go to school; each child has had his or her own alarm clock since the day they heard their first school bell.

WHEN WORK IS PLAY

My redheaded nephew Jared, who just turned three, often says, "My help!" when his mom, Madelyn, says she needs to do the laundry or wash the dishes. Jared likes to sit on the dryer and toss the dirty clothes in the washer as Madelyn hands them to him from the hamper. She measures out the detergent, and he dumps it in. To "help" wash dishes, Jared sometimes pulls his chair up to the kitchen sink, then scrubs dishes in the bubbles (many of them already clean and set on the counter).

Jared also likes to be a little handyman. Says Madelyn, "I was hanging a bulletin board and had gotten out the hammer and a nail when Jared noticed what I was doing. He immediately said, 'My help!' and ran and got his plastic toy hammer and wrench. I started the nail, then I had him bang on it with his own hammer. I said, 'Let me finish it off' and did the real hammering, then hung the bulletin board." Jared proudly proclaimed to Charlie, his daddy, "*My* help Mommy!"

PRAISE WORDS

Instead of praising physical attributes, intelligence, or skills, try praising your child for character traits associated with being a good worker.

Responsibility: "Tony, that was very responsible of you to put your toys away without my asking!"

Helpfulness: "You are being so helpful right now! I like it when you do the dishes with me."

Respect: "I noticed how careful you were not to interrupt my conversation with my friend. I'm glad you showed us respect."

Independence: "Sarah, you are so independent! You put your shirt on by yourself!"

But the little guy's help is not always pretend. Together, he and Charlie built a trellis out of PVC pipe for a hydroponic garden to grow tomatoes.

Small children not only *learn* by helping parents with chores; it also makes them feel great about themselves. Take advantage of that! As they grow older, they often become less enthusiastic about doing household jobs. Your kids are also likely to test you, to see how much you will let slide by when they aren't *quite* as helpful or responsible as usual.

MINIMIZING BAILOUTS

It's not always easy, even when you're determined to let your kids work things out for themselves responsibly and independently, to let them suffer the consequences if they don't. That's especially true if your children risk a major problem if you don't help them.

Parents have plenty of opportunities to bail kids out when they procrastinate or are forgetful. However, the more we do just that, the more our kids tend to rely on us. If your child forgets his lunch, his hunger pangs will remind him not to forget it the next day. I recommend not rescuing your kids from their mistakes too often. You'll find that on the rare occasion that you do, they'll practically bow down and kiss your feet.

One day last summer, Tyler knew I had a very heavy work schedule. I'd made it clear that to get to his driver's education

---

Dependability: "I'm so grateful that you have been dependable about taking the recycling out every week without my asking!"

Hard work: "Wow! You picked up all those puzzle pieces already? What a hard worker you are!"

Patience: "As soon as I finish vacuuming, we'll read a story, okay? You are being very patient."

Cheerfulness: "Your cheerful attitude sure made getting our chores done more fun!"

Creativity: "That's a creative approach to making your bed!"

Determination: "It took some determination to finish cleaning your guinea pig's cage; I know it's no fun."

class, he had to take the bus. He tried but missed it by a hair. Hmm. To bail him out or *not* to bail him out, that was the question. It was *very* hard for me to sit there, working in my office, knowing that if he missed the class we'd be out the money it cost us.

Nevertheless, I waited him out, offering no solutions. I typed away casually, overhearing him call other kids in his class, whom I could tell had already left. I reached for my car keys just as Tyler came in and sheepishly asked for a ride . . . but offered me free baby-sitting for Elisa that afternoon in exchange for the work time I'd lose having to drive him. I had to admit I was impressed—and glad I hadn't jumped too soon!

ALLOWANCES AND OTHER REWARDS

In our family, the purpose of giving our children allowances is not to directly pay them for chores, although they often see it that way. We tell them that as part of the family, we want them to share in our family finances and learn how to budget. In return, they're expected to help keep the family household running smoothly. We don't want to get in a position where our children expect to be paid for everything they do to help around the house. However, sometimes in addition to their weekly chores, they're given the option of earning more with specific jobs. For Tyler, that has included helping change the oil in the car or power-washing the driveway.

Every family is different, but in our family the amount of allowance we give varies according to the child's age and his or her ability to manage money. The big kids like the freedom to use allowance money for swimming or movies they go to without us. (If they go with us, we treat—a special perk for being willing to risk being seen with family by peers. They have to sit with us but don't have to hold our hands, unless they want popcorn . . . hee hee!) The kids are expected to use their own money to buy birthday gifts for friends and family. For generous and popular Aimee, that often means there's little left for anything else, but she is learning how to find bargains so she can have some cash left over for herself!

PARENTAL SELF-DISCIPLINE
AND RESPONSIBILITY

Confession time. I've learned from personal experience that when I'm not disciplined myself and the house becomes overwhelmingly messy, it's very hard for me to stop and play. It takes discipline for me to get my primary chores done. When I have an overwhelming workload or an injury, planning for and supervising help requires discipline and energy in itself.

I really feel for the kids when I get them on track but *I* get off track. My kids are expected to get their dirty clothes to me by laundry day, then later they have to take their clean clothes to their rooms and put them away. (They can do some wash themselves, but this way I *never* iron a single thing because I shake clothes out fresh from the dryer.) If they don't bring me the laundry baskets or their dirty clothes, they don't get clean clothes the following week. (Fortunately, the teen and preteen do care about clothing cleanliness!) However, when *I'm* guilty of missing laundry day, I frustrate my children. I have to be accountable to them.

Despite my terrifically responsible kids, no one who knows me well considers dropping in on us expecting to find an immaculate household. One of my close friends joked that she'd never known I had a kitchen counter until I swept off the clutter in her honor. It's not unusual for me to warn guests which bathrooms *not* to use. And I'm afraid that bed making drops low on the list of priorities. But is it really worth nagging (including nagging myself) when, despite our messy rooms, we never miss turning in our school or work assignments on time? I know I should teach my kids to keep their rooms cleaner—at least clean enough that we don't trip on something on the way to tucking them in at night. But doesn't it comfort you to know we are *not* a perfect family?

I must admit that there is a pitfall to raising responsible kids: It's easy to take advantage of the time they save us by working more instead of playing more. It takes some discipline to plan play activities, to reward jobs well done, and to take a break from all that responsibility!

COLOR PICKUP
Get a little help with tidying up by asking your child to pick up and put away all the blue items. Next do the red, then the yellow, then things bigger than his fist, then things smaller . . . until the room is clean!

TOOTH TRICKS
Try these creative tricks to encourage thorough toddler toothbrushing:

Serenade Me: While your tot sings "Aaaaa," brush her back teeth; "Eeeeee" gets the front.

Meal Review:
You: "What did you eat today?"
Your Child: "Ummm, a hot dog!"
You: "Okay, ten brushstrokes for the hot dog. One, two, three . . . What else did you eat?"
(Your two-year-old may want to brush all evening to " 'member everything!")

Toothbrush Tunes: Reserve a fun song for toothbrushing time, and have your child keep brushing until you sing to the very end of it.

LAUNDRY LESSONS
Shared chores offer multiple opportunities to teach children basic skills!
Clothes go *in* and *out* of the washer and dryer.
Count and sort them by *large and small, light and dark, same and different* (socks). You can also teach color and pattern identification.
Remember that your child is still too short to see everything. Teach *cause and effect* by lifting him up and letting him pull out starter knobs. Build conversation skills by talking about what you're doing.

chapter 11

Getting the Most from Toys, Games, and Other Play Tools

Toys are tools for you to use or lose! Here's what

to look for when choosing toys for your child.

"Mom, can we play Candy Land? *Please?*" My eyes glazed over at the thought of playing that game for the umpteenth time.

Tyler and Aimee had already worn out our first game box. It had fallen apart at the seams, and the brightly colored cards were bent and faded. As I had thrown it away, I'd muttered aloud that Elisa (then three) could surely live without it, couldn't she? But Tyler's fourteen-year-old friend heard me and said plaintively, "*Every* kid needs Candy Land!" so I reluctantly bought a new game for Elisa for Christmas.

Once again I found myself impatiently drumming my fingers on the board with the rainbow-colored trail, desperately hoping for a Queen Frostine card so I could race to the end and out of candy country. I'd already tried my trick of stacking the deck—putting the picture cards in the top one-third. But Elisa was getting the good ones, and I the duds.

What is it, I wondered, *that makes this game so appealing to kids?* The image of a sweet fantasyland is no doubt a big draw. Willie Wonka's chocolate factory had the same appeal. I doubt Candy Land would have lasted since 1949 had it been called Liver and Spinach Land. Also, it makes small children feel quite clever playing board games just like Mom and Dad, and it excites them to recognize colors and practice counting skills. And there's the suspense: Will the next card send you back to Plumpy, to start *all over* again?

For me, suspense had long ago given way to yawns. So I decided to try a new version with Elisa. At first, this meant our little gingerbread place markers, when passing each other on the board, shook their plastic hands and had very fine, squeaky, conversations with each other. Then I hit on Color I-Spy: Draw a card, then find an object in the room containing a matching color—no repeating objects. (For purple and orange, we looked on CD covers.)

This is a great way to play a table game with a wiggly child! Cruising the room for matching objects requires movement and imagination, even vocabulary building ("Look, Mom, there's some red on that globe in South America!"). And—the best part of all— we now tend to continue the game only as long as we are *both* having fun.

As you can see, adapting games in creative ways is one way you can enjoy them more. But you may find that helping your child understand the basic use of toys or games, and stimulating his imagination, also makes games more fun. In fact, *you* may make all the difference in how much enthusiasm your child develops for a toy and how much he learns while playing with it.

PARENT POWER

When Tyler was about two and a half, I gave him a box of Duplo building blocks. Oh, the possibilities in those yellow, blue, and red squares and rectangles! But I quickly discovered that my saying, "Why don't you play with your blocks?" then emptying them on the floor for him, was not enough to stimulate his interest.

He rarely played with them for more than a few minutes. I quickly tired of picking up blocks or nagging him to do it. I also tired of tripping over strays or finding blocks mixed in the toy box with McDonald's toys. Those blocks didn't seem worth the trouble! I thought, *Perhaps he's not old enough to play with them yet, or it's not in his area of interest.*

One day, I decided to spend fifteen minutes playing with the blocks *with* Tyler. As we played, I made comments like the following:

"See how these stick together better if you line the bumps up with the holes?"

"How about if I stack the blue ones while you stack the red?"

"Do you know that if you make a strong base, like this, you can make a higher tower that won't fall over?"

"Oooh! Look how high it is!"

Together we made a tower taller than him. We clapped and cheered. It leaned recklessly yet stood long enough for me to take a picture of Tyler standing next to it.

He had practiced identifying colors and counting while building. He discovered that by deliberately using wider pieces at the bottom, it would make his tower more stable. He said with pride, "*I'm* ma-kin' a base!" When he became thoroughly occupied with the blocks, I slipped away to do household chores. Hours later, after finally giving up block playing to go to bed, he fell asleep clutching one of his precious towers.

I was amazed to realize that only a few minutes of my time had turned a formerly dull activity into a favorite. It also made cleaning up more worthwhile. Tyler simply needed a few specific tips, an occasional extra hand, and some applause for his efforts.

Your interaction with your child is required in order for him to get the most out of his toys; gadgets cannot be expected to be baby-sitters, at least not for long.

TOY SELECTION

With the glut of toys on the market, how can you choose the best for your child? In my mind, the best toys or games are safe, plus they have several or all of the following features related to play value. The best toys:

⑨ can be played with in a variety of ways and stimulate some imagination.

⊚ teach more than one skill.

⊚ appeal to several age groups.

⊚ encourage positive behavior and learning, versus objection-able behavior and thinking. (Some violent toys and games aren't worth the "skills" a child practices.)

⊚ are fun (for the child—and hopefully for the parent, too).

⊚ get frequent, long-term use and stimulate interest in independent play.

⊚ offer a window into what a child is thinking or feeling.

Toys that don't meet many of these qualifications can be a waste of money and do little but create clutter in your home.

I used to write toy reviews for a parenting magazine. Toy manufacturers (including Fisher-Price and PlaySkool) sent me boxes full of play materials to evaluate. That made me think more deeply about what was worth occupying space in my own kids' rooms and what I could justifiably recommend to my 250,000 readers.

Once when the UPS man delivered a huge box of toys for me to review, the neighbor kids were gathered in my yard. Reviewing the

POPULAR CHILDREN'S TOYS

Infants/Babies
Squeeze/squeak toys (when compressed, they should not fit entirely in the child's mouth)
Nonbreakable mirrors
Rattles and teething toys
Cardboard books about baby animals
Large grip balls (no tiny rubber ones)
Activity quilts
Sturdy tub toys
Large blocks and nesting cups

Toddlers
Riding toys (keep away from stairs)
Musical toys
Push-pull toys
Chunky crayons

Puzzles with pieces that fit in individual holes (no sharp edges or points or pieces that might be ingested)
Toy telephones
Toy hammer

Preschoolers
Real tricycles
More complex art materials and puzzles
Role-playing with dolls and dollhouses
Puppets
Play kitchens with child-sized dishes
Child's tape player (batteries not easily accessible; don't allow near water)
Magnetic shapes for magnet boards
Toy figures
Construction toys

toys became a group project. The kids had fun giving them the Ebert & Roeper treatment. One thumbs-down preschool toy was designed so poorly it made us all laugh. A catapult was supposed to launch plastic treats (with numbers on them) into a creature's plastic mouth. Theoretically, it was designed to teach a child recognition of the numbers one through five. Realistically, correctly loading and launching the catapult required the motor skills of a kid who could count to fifty.

Of course, my creative crowd found other things to launch with the toy until the catapult fell off, so it wasn't a total bomb. I think toy manufacturers might be shocked at the innovative—*ahem*—ways children sometimes use toys. My son and his elementary-school cohorts took one look at an inflatable minitrampoline designed for preschoolers, turned it on its side . . . and attempted to roll each other down the street in it! It was a basically fun, safe product, designed for children ages two to six, who could jump inside the protective barrier. But it was oh-too-tempting for rowdy older children, and monitoring it created excessive wear and tear on my nerves.

If you're a new parent, you may have a tough time determining how much play value a toy offers. It might be a good idea to ask some experienced parents what their favorite toys have been for their own children, and why. Their experiences may apply to you as well, unless your children have drastically different personalities and abilities.

But when you're in a toy store and you hold an unfamiliar toy in your hand, what can you look for?

For starters, read the age recommendations on the package. Manufacturers base those on four factors:

1. The physical abilities required to manipulate a toy
2. The mental skills required so the child knows how to use it
3. Interests and play needs common to that age group
4. Most importantly, safety aspects

In other words, you can't go on developmental ability alone. Your highly advanced two-year-old may know his alphabet yet still choke on tiny, alphabet-shaped refrigerator magnets.

Will following the guidelines on the package ensure safety for your child? No. Believe it or not, many brand-new toys are already on their way to being recalled—or have already been recalled but not yet removed from store shelves. You can check on new and used toys by calling the Consumer Products Safety Commission at (800) 638-2772.

For now, however, let's continue to focus on play value.

TO BUY OR NOT TO BUY?

Any toy that merely requires a child to push a button to hear music or even phonics sounds is likely to have limited play value. Electronic toys are often overpriced and children tend to quickly lose interest in toys that don't require much skill on their part.

That doesn't mean I would never own such a thing. I might spare a whole two dollars for a *used* flashy thingamajig. And I rarely thumb my nose at gifts given to my kids, although even gifts must eventually adequately justify the space they take and the mess they make.

When Elisa was a year old, she was given a little "radio" that played music when a button was pushed. Although she quickly outgrew the toy, she certainly enjoyed it and would hum along with the tunes. Strangely enough, instead of using her hand to push the button, she would turn on the toy by smacking it against her forehead. Imagine the sight of a wispy-haired half-pint, toddling around while alternately humming and smacking her head whenever the music stopped. It was hilarious! I figure that anything that adds a little humor to life—and a funny memory—gets an extra point for play value.

Many beeping, buzzing, flashing toys that children end up begging for are ones that have appeared on TV commercials. The toys appear much more impressive on the tube, of course. Give in and buy them and you'll find many soon lose their appeal and end up in the mishmash in the bottom of the toy box.

To avoid excess or impulse spending, especially when kids beg, I recommend the following strategies:

Strategy #1: Wait

By waiting several months to a year, even after agreeing it might be a potential Christmas or birthday present, you can find out how long-term or short-lived your child's eagerness for a toy may be. Eagerness often wanes when a child realizes it may be his only Christmas or birthday present, and other toys become more enticing. If nothing else, the child learns that delayed gratification is okay.

Strategy #2: Put It on "The List"

The List can be on a real piece of paper or in your head. The next time your child points at a toy and asks, "Can I have that?" you might reply enthusiastically, "Not today. But you can put it on your list!" That list is made up of toys your child wants you to choose from when you pick his birthday gift, or toys he may choose to buy himself with money he earns. Personally, I'm a real stickler for giving gifts only for special occasions. (I'll explain why in strategy #3.)

There's something very magical about The List. My kids have asked with excitement, "Can I put anything I want on it?" My answer is usually yes, if it is within reason. If I have no intention of ever buying that toy, or even letting the child buy it himself, I will say no firmly. I might do this if the toy is outrageously expensive or it is objectionable in some way. If it simply looks like it offers low play value, I put it on the list but later may persuade the kid to recognize for himself that it lacks value.

It can be useful to go to a toy store with no intent to purchase anything that day for your child (you may need a birthday gift for your child's friend or cousin) but with perfect willingness to make lists. Some kids love all kinds of lists, so it can become a fun activity all in itself! Often, within minutes of a child putting a favored item on The List, she forgets about it altogether. The simple creation of the list has become a form of parent-child play!

You may also find that creating lists for your child causes you to think twice yourself about the difference between what *you* need and want, and how willing you are to delay gratification yourself. I was amused when in a toy store I overheard another mother saying to her daughter, "Oh, you'd like to have that? Put it on your list!" I told her that we use lists too. The woman laughed, telling me it backfired on her once. She wanted to buy scrapbooking supplies for herself. Guess what her daughter told her? "Put it on *your* list, Mommy!"

I hope you will also use opportunities to talk to your child about why he feels he needs certain toys. Remind him frequently that we don't truly *need* playthings to make us happy. You can demonstrate (as you've seen in previous chapters in this book) that much fun can be made out of thin air, no spending required. Of course, that's a lesson adults need to learn—and relearn, and relearn!

Strategy #3: Let the Child Work for It

When a child knows he needs to save his allowance, break a habit, or do extra chores to be able to purchase a toy, that toy may instantly become less appealing. That often applies even if Mom or Dad offers to pay half. Ten dollars of your money may not seem like much to him. But five dollars of his, well that's another story! The same goes for doing chores—one day is fine, but weeks?

When three-and-a-half-year-old Elisa decided to empty the dishwasher every day for four weeks so she could earn her stuffed animal, it was a sacrifice to her, but she was determined. As you saw in the previous chapter, very young children can often grasp the concept of working towards long-term goals—including goals to break (or form) long-term habits.

You might also be surprised to discover how attached a child becomes to a toy he has earned or paid for himself. The strong association with achieving a goal, or the memory of walking up to a counter to pay for something "all by myself!" with money the child truly earned may cause a child to hang on to that toy long after it has been outgrown. Why? It becomes part of a child's life story, his record of accomplishments, instead of a mere plaything.

Elisa can quickly pick out from her pile of stuffed animals the little Saint Bernard she earned. Whenever she spends her allowance, she loves to tell strangers, "I bought this with my own money I earned emptying the dishwasher!" She's consistently rewarded by strangers' responses: "Really? You do that all by *yourself?*"

Tyler and I took a trip down memory lane recently when he moved into a new bedroom and in the process shed many of his childhood possessions in favor of a more teen-friendly pad. Around the same time, he told me, "Hey, you want to know something funny? I met a guy at lunch today who had a Ninja Turtle water bottle too!" As a sixteen-year-old, he could still recall working hard at age three to earn that!

Don't let your generosity with your children deny them the pleasure of earning, and the thrill of enjoying, toys they can work for.

Strategy #4: Use Toy Purchasing to Teach Financial Planning

The excitement of toy shopping can be a fun shared activity. But not every moment is fun, especially if you want to teach your child some fiscal responsibility. Once a preschooler can count her cash and can stomp her feet and insist, "I have my own money!" you must decide whether or not you will allow her to make an unwise decision.

I had this very dilemma once when Elisa had amassed a whopping twenty-seven dollars (birthday-gift money and six weeks' worth of two-dollar allowances). What a wad of cash for a five-year-old! Of course, there had been moments when she had wanted to spend portions before but hadn't had her wallet with her.

Finally she stood, wallet in hand, stubbornly holding a too-expensive toy that she actually could afford: a pretend pet carrier stuffed with veterinary supplies and a stuffed animal to doctor. We tried to dissuade her. We fanned out her dollar bills, telling her it would use it *all,* that she could get two toys for the price of one with that money.

"I don't care! It's my money," she cried out. I told her there was a good chance we might find the exact same toy elsewhere for less money. She didn't care. She was determined not to walk out that door empty-handed.

At that point I had to make an executive decision. I told her that I would not let her buy it right then. But I promised her that that very day, I would call to check prices in other stores, and she could buy the toy that evening, either there or elsewhere. I told her that part of my job as Mom is to teach her how to manage her money responsibly. I promised I would bring her back later that evening if that was the best price we could find for the toy.

She was pretty disgruntled about the whole thing. Then Aimee offered to buy her a token gift for a few bucks after Elisa chose to let go of the Big Toy, so her little sister didn't have to leave the store empty-handed. That led to a funny conversation with the teenage store clerk, who overheard Aimee and I say a few times, "Can we buy you this?" with Elisa replying, "No." The teen said she'd never heard a parent begging to buy a child a toy, with the child refusing!

GROWN-UP GAMES MADE EASY

UNO (Mattel). For three-year-olds, eliminate most of the rules. Stick only with recognizing and matching colors.

TO PLAY: Lay all cards that have been dealt to each person faceup on the table. Follow the typical progression of play by laying down a card (say, a blue card with a number 3 on it). Have the child match the color (but not the number) with one of his own cards. After he catches on and has learned some number recognition, he can match numbers, too. Later, you can add the Reverse cards (reversing the direction of play with more than two people) to help your child learn right-left discrimination. I use the Draw Four cards, but I don't force a child to lose his turn. As dexterity increases, a child can fan and conceal cards.

Verbalize your own problem solving to encourage creative thinking in your child. For instance, you might say, "You have ten cards left. I have only two. In this game, you will win if you can get rid of all your cards first." You can suggest, "If you put down a yellow card, and I only have red ones, I can't get rid of a card—I have to draw more!"

Monopoly (Parker Brothers). Start with place markers, dice, and property cards only. (Hide the cute little houses and hotels if you want to eliminate distractions.)

TO PLAY: Each player rolls the dice, counts the dots, and moves the marker the correct number of spaces. He "wins" the property he lands on. (As adults we have played this way with a Norwegian version of the game!) He gets to find the matching property card from the stack; first he looks for the correct color, then for the first few letters in the property name. The player with the most cards wins. Later, increase the game's complexity by awarding money only for passing Go and paying rent to property-card owners. (Lots of one-dollar bills makes counting out rent easier.)

To be honest, this whole lesson turned out far better than I thought it would. We found the exact same toy for five dollars cheaper at another store, and in that one, the dog was her favorite breed—a dalmatian! Since then, Elisa and I have been doctoring stuffed animals together in our makeshift animal hospital, and discussions about her fine financial decision continue.

Strategy #5: Consider Buying Playthings Used

I confess. I'm a cheapskate. Or I'm a master bargain hunter, depending on how you look at it. Toys your kids want but that are too costly for you can often be found used. It's wise not to ignore safety issues, of course; examine toys carefully for broken or loose pieces (especially when the toy will be used by babies or toddlers).

Scrabble (Milton Bradley Company). Set out all the letters faceup, instead of facedown.

TO PLAY: Have your child think of any word he wants. Help him sound it out phonetically, find the necessary letters, and spell it on the game board. Each new word should connect to the last. Then you can make up a silly story together with the words, pointing to them as you say them. As your child is able, increase complexity by dealing out random letters. He must then think of a word starting with one of his letters, but can trade others to finish that word. When he's older, he can learn to play the traditional way, which limits him to letters drawn randomly.

Master Mind (Pressman). This less-familiar game is a winner for practicing problem-solving skills, fine motor control (pincher grasp in the fingers), and eye-hand coordination. The mini version is excellent for car travel. Preschoolers love to create patterns by pushing the colored pegs into holes in the box.

TO PLAY: Hide four pegs (all one color) behind the barrier. Your child will try to guess your hidden color by placing corresponding colored pegs in the first row. If she's incorrect, you give clues. "Not right yet—which colors haven't you tried?" Subsequent guesses are made in subsequent rows. All previous guesses are left in place, so the child (1) reflects on what's already been tried and (2) uses the process of elimination to come to new conclusions. (These are valuable skills your child can't learn too soon!) Once these concepts are grasped, complexity of color combinations can be increased. For example, instead of using four red pegs, you can use two blue, a red, and a white. You can also increase the complexity of your clues: "You have all the right colors, but only two are in the right spots. Try rearranging them."

You may want to call to be sure a toy hasn't been recalled by the manufacturer. But you can find incredible bargains on very durable play equipment.

One of my great finds was a plastic molded preschool desk, for a quarter of its original price, at a children's store that sold used clothing. Another was a foot-operated, toddler-sized car, marked FREE by a parent and placed on the sidewalk because a wheel had come off. I simply ordered a replacement wheel on-line, directly from the manufacturer, and voilà! It came in the mail a few days later.

The Salvation Army is a great place to buy table games. You can also find used toys via the Internet. When Elisa was three, she became obsessed with having a toy guitar. She had seen it repeatedly in a commercial that played in a movie I'd bought her (a rather unfair trick to pull on a parent, I think). To "play" the guitar, a child needed only to insert a hand into a hole in the center, causing electronic music to play automatically.

I initially nixed buying the toy. The play value was obviously not in proportion to the steep price. I also suspected that the repetition of some of those songs might drive me off to la la land in a hurry. But Elisa's begging intensified when she saw the toy in toy aisles, and she kept insisting it be put on The List.

I finally agreed to buy it used if I could find it. I typed in the name of the toy and the word *used* in the search bar, and lo and behold, I found a mother selling one in our neighborhood.

As I had suspected, the toy was certainly *not* all it had cracked up to be. It turned out to be more of a showpiece for Elisa than anything else; her pleasure in the toy was proportional to the amount of envy it generated in visiting playmates. Aargh! Finally to my relief, and her complete delight, Elisa sold it herself at our garage sale—for three whole dollars! By now it is possibly a sixth-generation garage-sale toy, or perhaps it's buried in *your* toy box, covered with Duplos.

Strategy #6: Don't Rule out Nontoys
Some of the best "toys" are not labeled as such. One toddler favorite in our family was a set of twelve nesting gift/storage boxes. We

played with them as "toys" for quite a while. We stacked them and knocked them down. We gave stuffed animals rides in them. We took turns guessing under which box a ball was hidden (the old shell game). Finally I reluctantly decided to use them to store Christmas decorations. (For another nontoy idea, see Sugar-Cube Mystery on page 165.)

Strategy #7: Check Your Game Closet before Buying New Toys

Many toys or games designed for older children and adults can be adapted for use by toddlers and preschoolers. In addition to saving money, using grown-up versions of toys can make play much more interesting for you. Karen, mother of two, admits, "I don't like to play with toys that much. But I do like to do things with my children that really interest me. Annette and I have been playing geography games, including making up games with the atlas, since she was three. She [now seven] knows almost all the countries in Africa and Eastern Europe, all the continents, and so on. She's a whiz. It has been so much fun, because I love geography."

Also, since Annette has been in her elementary-school chess club, the whole family is learning to play chess. Karen says, regarding her five-year-old son, Matthew, "He beat me, fair and square! You should have seen how proud of himself he was. I had a blast." Karen wants other parents to know it's okay to do what you love, because through your own passion you can make it fun for your kids.

TOY USE

You can learn how to adapt toys and games in creative and educational ways to make them more fun and to fit various age groups and personality types. Sometimes this adaptation comes spontaneously from children with differing ages and personalities. All you have to do is sit back and watch!

As Tyler grew, and our box of Duplos passed from one child to the next, I saw those blocks used in various creative ways. My kids rarely built anything with them in the traditional manner, other than a few simple houses. But they invented dozens of ways to play with them unrelated to stacking! From sorting sizes and colors, to making a brick road for small cars, to creating a maze in which salamanders could run, my kids' creativity amazed me. As for cleanup, we'd play "basketball," racing against time and each other to toss the blocks into the bucket.

It was also interesting to observe my kids' Duplo personalities. Tyler consistently made towers of single colors, with blocks all the same size. That was consistent with his organized, logical mind. Aimee randomly mixed colors and sizes, and she continues to favor variety.

But sometimes it takes deliberate planning. You must stop and think, *What does this game or toy teach? What can I use it to teach?* Your child may need your inventiveness and experience to know what to do with a toy.

One of my favorite toys has been a puzzle/play mat made of interlocking, flat, spongy, three-inch squares (about a half-inch thick). The squares are part of a large puzzle. When put together with the right number of squares across, they create a large floor mat. But within each square is a spongy letter that can be pressed out, then put back in the correct hole, creating a puzzle within each square.

This is a toy that has met all my qualifications for a toy with high play value, especially when used with a parent. Once again, I'm going to list toy features to look for to help imprint them in your mind. I'll use the alphabet sponge blocks to illustrate.

It can be played with in a variety of ways. Aside from pressing the blocks together in a row with the letters in order, or creating a play mat from them, you can:

- Connect six squares to make a block; make more to stack and topple
- Build the sides of a castle with the pieces flat or in blocks

- In the bath, float the spongy letters or stick them on the side of the tub
- Create paths to traipse along or drive toy cars on
- Draw a letter out of a bag, and have your child think of a word starting with that phonics sound
- Trace around the letters or use them for sponge painting

It teaches more than one skill. Those skills include problem solving; color, letter, and number identification; texture recognition (recognizing the bumpy fronts of the puzzle pieces versus the smooth backs to get the letters in correctly); and phonics.

It appeals to several age groups. In addition to using the puzzle pieces with toddlers and preschoolers, we showed them to four-week-old Elisa, who was mesmerized by them. I would assemble the puzzle and prop it up in front of her infant seat. Her eyes danced around the images. When she was old enough to lie on her stomach and rest on her elbows, we laid her on the mat, and she would feel the textures with her fingers while looking at the colorful letters. Before she had teeth she was allowed to chew on them.

With five-year-old Aimee, I assembled a few letter blocks. She would find additional ones to create various words to spell and read. And at the far end of the age spectrum, I have used the blocks myself, without any kids! When giving a message for a writers' group and using an acrostic to convey my points, I gradually attached each letter until the puzzle pieces spelled out the theme of my speech.

This toy has encouraged positive behavior and learning. How can you beat teaching a kid to read?

It's fun; gets frequent, long-term use; and stimulates interest in independent play. We're on our tenth year with this toy and it looks the same as the day I got it. I'm almost ready to pass it on to my nephews, but not yet!

It offers a window into what a child is thinking. It's a thrill to realize that not only does a child recognize letters, but she also can spell words on her own.

GAME ADAPTATION

There is rarely a *right* way to play with a toy or play a game. Although we want to teach our children good sportsmanship in learning to follow game rules, some flexibility has value as well. It can be wonderfully freeing to realize that you can take simple concepts the toys teach and expand on those concepts. I much prefer to adapt adult versions of games than to purchase short-lived preschool versions.

When your preschooler spies a shelf of table games geared for adults or older kids, then cries out, "Mommy, I want to play *those!*" is this a problem or an opportunity? Many games designed for grown-ups can be adapted for use with little ones. Unlike games created only for preschoolers, these won't be outgrown. While playing modified adult table games, your child learns and practices complex skills and enjoys feeling more "grown up."

The key is to appropriately adapt games to your child's skill level and developmental age. To do this, eliminate some rules, or create new games with game pieces and boards you already own. Even a standard deck of cards can be used for color-, suit-, and number-matching games. Provide enough challenge, but keep it fun. Decide on new rules ahead of time (lest a new game should develop—that of continually altering rules). Put game pieces you won't use out of sight. (For tips on adapting UNO, Monopoly, Scrabble, and Mastermind, see sidebar on pages 156–157.)

PLAY-MATERIAL STORAGE

How you store toys in your household is largely a matter of taste and space in your home. I have tried dozens of methods and continue to experiment, depending on the age of my children. I confess that I'm not consistently good about making sure toys are picked up. It's hard to be firm when my own papers and clothes are not always picked up as they should be! Nevertheless, I've learned some lessons over the years. The following are some tips that will help your child remain interested in his toys longer and encourage him to play with them independently as well as with you. These tips are also likely to decrease mess and frustration for you. Just remember to do as I say and not as I do.

Store items with small parts out of sight—and possibly out of reach. Keep toys like blocks, dollhouse accessories, toy tools, or fake food in bins in the closet or in drawers. This will decrease frustration for your child when friends come to play who have a tendency to dump and run. It will also help your child feel less confused and overwhelmed by clutter.

When my kids have friends over, their guests are expected to help with pickup. Sometimes it's not practical, such as when the playmate's parent comes to the door to pick up Junior and her engine is running. In that case, my own child must pick up the mess left by his guest. It's part and parcel of having "company," just as I do dishes after serving cake to my own company. Just because my child begged to have a friend over doesn't mean I have to clean up after him! (That applies to teens who spill soda pop on the carpet as well!)

When children must deliberately ask for toys with small parts and are asked to plan ahead to include cleanup in their play, several things happen. For one, the toy becomes more appealing, especially if it has been out of their field of vision for a while. Think about how you feel when you pull out a box of winter clothes and find a favorite sweater you haven't looked at for a year. You tend to be reminded of why you liked it in the first place!

Also, use of a toy that has been out of sight for a while turns into more of a special event, especially when you enthusiastically say, "Hey, let's have a block day!" (or a "puppet day"). Get on the floor with your child and model creative uses of the toy. Before you know it, you might find yourself shooed away and the toy played with for hours by the child, especially if you show a lot of enthusiasm for it!

Store items near the area where you want them used, or where you will be frequently reminded to use them. If you want art supplies used in the kitchen, store them there. This not only makes it easier to do projects, but it prevents visiting children from decorating the carpet in the playroom with markers or paint. Store musical instruments (maracas, a tambourine, etc.) somewhere near the stereo, and you'll stimulate some impromptu performances. Keep a supply of good children's books near a comfy reading chair.

Try to set up small areas throughout your home for individual activities. Many day-care centers do this, and preschoolers respond well to it.

Store items your child uses often in a place that's accessible to her. My kids have always loved doing art projects. From toddlerhood on my kids have had their own art drawers to dip into whenever they wanted. They have spent hour upon hour drawing pictures, and they often gravitate to their little art section when bored. Five-year-old Elisa once surprised me by showing me a scrapbook page she'd created entirely on her own, made from photos I'd given her a few months before.

Sometimes a brief comment from you might stimulate your child's imagination and send him running to his art center. One day I was in the kitchen cooking when I commented that I had an over-abundance of spaghetti noodles. Perhaps they could be used for a project—say, as kitty whiskers? I continue to make dinner, and less than ten minutes later (no kidding) Elisa tapped on my shoulder to show me the cat she had made. She had cut a cat head shape out of construction paper, drawn features, and glued on noodle whiskers. Wow! I had her dictate directions for the project she had invented, and I wrote them down for her (extending the independent play into parent-child play). The next day she showed her preschool class how to make cats with noodle whiskers!

Now, I know you're probably laughing at me because you're remembering the story of Elisa drawing on the wall. But as you can tell, that incident did not cause me to mistrust my child with art materials. She continued to have her own accessible supply, which she has never misused since. When on some occasions she has accidentally made a mess—for instance, underestimating how much glue will come out of a container—she has hollered for me. However, hours of independent play and creativity (stimulated by a child being able to reach her own materials) more than make up for an occasional mess.

In summary, wisely chosen, used, and stored play materials can be great tools for stimulating independent play as well as parent-child play. And as you will see in our next chapter, they can even be used to help give your child a well-rounded education.

5 minute fun

SUGAR-CUBE MYSTERY
(props needed: sugar cubes, pencil, glass of water)

"Tell me what letter or number you want me to write on this sugar cube."

"Um . . . how 'bout an A, like my name starts with?"

Write that letter in pencil, rather darkly, on the sugar cube. Pick it up between your thumb and forefinger, with your thumb pressing hard against the letter you drew (but don't let your child see that it transfers the pencil mark to your thumb). Drop the sugar cube into a glass of water, and quickly grasp your child's hand to set it over the top of the glass. As you place his hand there, firmly push your thumb against your child's palm. This will transfer the letter to his hand. As he watches the sugar cube dissolve, say, "Let's see if the letter rises up out of the water and onto your hand!" Then have him look at his hand.

Preschoolers find this so fascinating that even when kids know how it works they want you to do it again and again—to everyone at their birthday party!

BOWLING FUN
When we moved and had to live in a bare house for about a month, we had to invent a lot of our own fun. In desperation, we made long rolls with blankets to create a bowling alley. We set up empty plastic liter bottles at the end of the room, then we rolled a Tinker-toy can down our "alley" to knock them down!

HUMAN BUBBLE
When your child is in the bathtub, take in a container of bubbles. (The no-spill bubble containers work best because the bubble solution won't get lost too quickly.) Using the wand, blow big bubbles onto the surface of the water. If your child's skin and your hands are wet enough, you can transfer the bubbles from the surface of the water to his body.

By the way, bubble bath makes a great beard. Bring a hand mirror into the bathroom so your child can see himself and laugh.

chapter 12

abc and do-re-mi

Using Play to Teach

How marvelous it is to see a child learn something

new! How joyfully rewarding it is to see him learn

from you as you play together!

L et's play categories!" said Tyler, as I pushed him on the swing in our yard.

"Okay. What category?" I asked.

"How 'bout the letter *B?*"

"Okay. But instead of just saying words that start with *B,* let's say them each time I give the swing a push."

As the swing came toward me, Tyler giggled and yelled out, "Bubbles!"

I pushed him hard and high to give myself thinking time . . . and as it swung back towards me I said, "Ball!"

"Baby!" Tyler quickly replied . . . and we played until we ran out of *B* words (I ran out, actually), then we chose another alphabet letter. To Tyler, it was pure fun. To me, it was serious fun; he was practicing phonics—the early building blocks of reading!

At that time, I remember wondering, *Why does Tyler enjoy letters and words so much?* Was it because he'd seen me putting words to paper since the day he was born? Or maybe it was because we'd been reading stories together, every single evening, from the time he was a baby. Tyler discovered early on that those strange marks could create colorful, active images in our minds. He also associated our story times with warm snuggling.

When Tyler first asked what the marks on the pages were called, I gave him a puzzle containing the letters in his name. Shortly thereafter, when he saw an EXIT sign, he yelled out ecstatically, "Look! My *E!*" Encouraged by his excitement, I bought a puzzle with all the alphabet letters. We sang the alphabet song while touching the individual pieces. Later, Tyler invented games with refrigerator magnet letters. He'd ask me to remove one and move the rest around when he was not looking. Then he'd guess which letter was missing.

That was followed by a determination to write letters himself. At that point I wondered, *Shouldn't he learn all the letters and sounds before writing them—and from a qualified teacher? Did I know what I was doing?* I had not made any conscious decision to teach him to read. I simply loved language myself, so teaching him what an alphabet letter looked like—and eventually what it sounded like—seemed no different from showing him how to hold a spoon, or throw a ball, or put on his own socks.

Most of the time I was responding to his own eager questions, which often came when I was preoccupied in the kitchen or office.

"Mom! How do you make an *H?*"

"Two sticks with a line across them."

"What does Dad start with?"

"D"

Eventually, instead of saying, *"D,"* I'd say, "It makes the *duh* sound. What letter do you think that is?" To be honest, I began teaching my son phonics early because I quickly tired of having to spell words for him. Yet that also added a thrill of discovery, which my son found irresistible.

As Tyler grew, we continued to play word games, language games, and reading games. As I watched him grow and learn, I began to wonder if purposeful play could positively affect *all* types of learning.

Over the years that followed, I had the wonderful opportunity to teach not one, but *three* children through play. I've also had the opportunity to study what many experts have to say on the topic of learning. It has been rewarding to clearly see how teaching my kids through play has had a direct effect on their academic success, eagerness to learn, and study habits.

YOU'VE GOT THE POWER!

I assume that since you are reading this book, you are an involved parent. Your child can learn all kinds of things from you when his interest is stimulated and he is developmentally ready to process what you tell him. From the moment he points his finger and questions, "That?" or asks his first "Why?" or "How?" and you answer him, you are *teaching*.

As an adult, you have gained much wisdom, knowledge, and experience since you were a child yourself. All you need in order for your child to learn from you is willingness to:

- Be with your child
- Explore his interests with him and feed them
- Find out what he needs to know at his particular age
- Help him find and use the information he needs to know

I assume that you taught your child how to put on a coat, share his toys, and tie his shoes—and you probably felt some confidence in doing so. I'll bet you taught him words for things too, to help him learn to talk. I'm willing to bet that most of what your child learned as a toddler, he learned from you or other family members. But once your child reached preschool age, did you continue to feel that confidence in your ability to teach your own child?

THE GREAT PRESCHOOL MYTH

There seems to be a perception among many parents that unless a child begins learning from professionals at an early age, he will not reach his full potential in his later academic years.

I see two misconceptions here. One is the belief that a parent is not capable of teaching a preschool child what he needs to know. You are fully capable of doing this, barring a mental disability of some kind. You may even be capable of teaching your child when he is older, if that option fits your and your children's personalities and academic goals.

Of course, we must recognize our limitations. I certainly could not teach my son his biochemistry (although Gordy could if he wanted to), but I seriously doubt that my son's English teacher or wrestling coach could teach him that either. No teacher must be all or do all—and neither must you. Even homeschooling parents often send their kids to public school for specific courses, or to homeschool workshops with other families. (One co-op in our area offers workshops on subjects from frog dissecting to language arts.)

Also, if your child is developmentally delayed in any way, getting expert help early on in a special-education preschool can make a big difference to him in the long run. However, such programs are most effective when parents follow through with activities at home, incorporating the teaching of skills into everyday activities (such as getting dressed) as well as parent-child play.

However, when it comes to preschool curriculum, I suspect you know your colors and your *ABCs*. Find out from your public school what a child is expected to know before entering kindergarten, and that should boost your confidence.

Another common misconception is that early teaching by professionals is necessary to help a child not only keep up with peers but surpass them. I've heard parents express worry about finding the best preschools so their children will get into elite kindergartens, ensuring that they will be prepared for the best colleges! Frankly, I think that's hogwash!

Not that I'm preschool bashing; I *love* preschool. Every one of my kids has enjoyed preschool. Your child may learn fascinating facts from a gifted preschool teacher. She may come home and tell you all about the rain-forest canopy—something you never *thought* to teach your child or maybe never even knew (but could learn with your child, from library books). I have tremendous respect for trained teachers and the impact they have on children. I feel grateful for the opportunities my children have enjoyed and for the time preschool has afforded me to focus on some of my own projects.

Without Elisa's marvelous preschool teachers, this book would not have been written! I'm grateful, too, for the fun, messy projects my children have done without me and for the renewed energy I've often felt after having a little time to myself. I love it that Elisa can play on play equipment a little without my having to supervise, and that she can learn how to communicate with other children in a group setting.

If you have a child in preschool, you may appreciate the same things. But please don't think that means you are incapable of teaching a preschooler or even an older child what he needs to know to be successful. I hope you can see that while I have tremendous respect for teachers, I also have tremendous respect for parents. Please don't discount the impact you can have on your child's ability to learn—and on *what* he can learn. The only real question is what you choose to teach him, and to what degree.

If nothing else, you can make use of opportunities to expand on what your child is learning in preschool. You may even have some funny, memorable conversations!

Elisa and her friend Abby were riding in the car one day, discussing what to use for "sharing time" that started with that week's letter, *W*. Elisa's toy veterinary kit would have worked for last week's letter, *V*, but not for the current week. Still, I reminded her, she had *wanted* the toy badly yet had *waited* to buy one at a better price—two *W* words.

Abby replied, "*One* starts with *W* too!"

"Actually," I smiled and said, "*one* starts with *O*. It's spelled *O-N-E*."

"But that should be *ohn,* not *one*." Clever girl—the *E* on the end makes the first vowel say its name, right? Well, not always . . .

To further confuse her, I added, "Guess what else: A word that sounds like *ohn* is actually spelled *O-W-N*."

"But that would be *ouwn!*" Right; it should!

THREE WAYS YOU CAN TEACH

I see three different levels of involvement when it comes to influencing what and how children learn. The first type of teaching occurs in the first years of your child's life. The other two can occur throughout his educational years.

1. Basic nurturing: guided support of a child's use of his innate abilities. For instance, encouraging a baby to learn to walk, and when he is older, allowing him to use a curb as a balance beam when you walk to the park.
2. Expanding on what a child has already learned: for example, helping a child apply what she's learning in a new way, or practicing what she has learned.
3. Teaching of new skills, facts, concepts, or methods: for instance, teaching a child phonics, algebra, or how to ride a bike.

When your child learns to walk, you don't "teach" him in the formal sense. You don't instruct him to move his legs and tell him how to bear weight on them. Instead, you provide a mix of freedom, safety, and encouragement, which urges him to practice a skill that gradually comes naturally. You clap, you cheer, you urge him to move toward your outstretched arms—to bravely try again when he takes a tumble.

To acquire basic skills, your infant or toddler will learn primarily by observing others and using the senses he was born with, although some children with disabilities need more practice to do what comes more naturally to others. In that case, you can learn from a treatment team (occupational therapists, physical therapists, speech therapists, vision therapists, etc.) how you can help your child in the area in which he struggles. You may even come up with some creative games of your own; you may begin to bridge the gap from basic nurturing to expanding on what a child is learning.

For example, my youngest struggled to pronounce *L*'s and *S*'s. This concerned me a bit, because speech had come more naturally to my first two. A speech therapist found my child to be a borderline case—she had a few problems, but the therapist thought they might disappear by elementary school.

Instead of constantly correcting my child when she was talking to us, I decided to try a few games. At that time, she was quite wiggly when I used a hair dryer on her hair, so she and I sang songs to keep her occupied and still. Consequently, it was easy—and fun— to sing silly songs with *S*'s and *L*'s. We watched each other's mouths in the mirror and laughed while saying, "Little Lola loved her lollipops!" My daughter could see in the mirror that "Wittow Wowa" looked a whole lot different from "Little Lola," so she gradually began to correct herself.

Honestly, when a child's thinking skills, social skills, motor skills, and speech all come along quite naturally—when everything works as it's supposed to—it is quite a miracle!

Take a look at the following list of skills a child is expected to begin mastering by the time he or she enters grade school. Most motor skills should come naturally to your child with your guided support. Some of the other skills will also develop on their own, although many social and thinking skills require a little more focused teaching and practice.

Motor skills. Your child will learn how to use both sides of his body together (called bilateral motor coordination). He will learn to distinguish his right hand from his left. He will also learn how to use his eyes to coordinate movement of his hands as he draws. (If a therapist needs to work with your child, she will call this visual-motor integration.)

Thinking skills. Your child will find ways to concentrate and focus, use memory, and recall directions. She will learn to generalize—to apply what she has learned to new situations or to categorize things. Your child will also learn, with practice, how to problem solve, make decisions, organize materials, follow logical steps, and evaluate what he's done. Wow!

Social skills. Your child will learn how to properly express his feelings with self-control. He will develop a vocabulary consistent with his developmental age and will learn to understand nonverbal signs and symbols (including reading). He will learn to watch others and recognize what behavior is appropriate and what's not, to compromise when negotiating, to cooperate or compete in a healthy way, and to set appropriate limits for himself and others. Double wow!

REMAIN AMAZED!

If you're aware of some of the skills an activity teaches, you're more likely to recognize small achievements as you play rather than focusing exclusively on an end product. The end result of a four-year-old's magazine collage is likely to be a collection of crookedly cut and placed pictures, with an overabundance of glue seeping out between them. Most kids that age can't cut perfectly straight with scissors.

And yet that same child may demonstrate a great mental leap by collecting pictures that are related in an unusual way or choosing a creative way to organize them on the page. Becoming more sensitive to the skills your child is learning or practicing will introduce a sense of wonder and excitement into your playtimes together. If the end result is something you don't want to hang on to forever, one solution is to take a picture of the finished product, and later you can toss the gluey mess.

Scrapbooking with photos is a project much like making magazine collages, but the results are more keeper friendly. A page with crookedly cut photos of a child roller-skating with Daddy—accompanied by her name scrawled with the letters backward—reflects not only the father-daughter memory but her developmental level at the time she went skating.

Elisa's finished scrapbook pages don't look like mine or her sister's. Occasionally I have to resist the urge to straighten a glued-down photo. But it fascinates me that she can already plan pages on specific themes. For instance, she had a few photos of friends' animals, so she decided to begin what she called her "dog page." She then asked to borrow my camera so she could take photos of two stuffed dogs. Over the course of the following week, she reminded me several times to get the film developed. When I finally did, she took the developed shots and cropped them to fit on her page of existing dog shots. She is using all of the thinking skills I mentioned above!

It fascinates me that she can already mentally crop photos. She sometimes asks for my help with the cropping machine, but her directions are very specific: "Mom, can you trim *this* much off the top and sides, leaving out the tree but including that building?" She even crops as she takes photos, using the zoom function on the camera! Her shots are so good we usually can't tell who took the pictures, she or I. The exception is with group shots of people, because rather hilariously, if you look closely, everyone she photographs instantly hunches over. They can't imagine that a three-and-a-half-foot peanut with a camera will actually get them all in the shot.

LEARNING TOOLS

As you can see, teaching a child often includes giving him tools and showing him how to use them. When he cries out in frustration because the scissors won't work, you show him how to use both sides of his body when cutting: one hand holds the paper, the other manipulates the scissors. *You* are helping your child practice bilateral motor coordination!

In addition to telling a child how to do something, part of learning is giving a child *tools* for learning. You might, in response to a child's question, say, "I don't know the answer, but let's find out together!" Teaching him how to find information can be more valuable than spoon-feeding him facts.

When Tyler was around three, he got his first library card. (Aimee had to wait a little longer, because she was more inclined to shuffle the contents of library shelves around than to read at that age.) Tyler was interested in cars and bugs, so I taught him how to do a subject search on the library computer, as the librarian had taught me. We then located the books on the shelves—acres of books on bugs and cars.

I still recall the look of wonder in his eyes. He said, "You can find out *anything* at the library!" I responded that generally, yes, you can, although the library does have its limitations. He caught on to that when he was older and found conflicting information in books about the *Amistad* slave ship. (The book based on the movie was a more romanticized, less accurate version than the original book.) His new lesson became how to discern which resources are most reliable and unbiased—a lesson he continues to learn, as do we all.

Another teaching tool is nearby exhibits or workshops at science or history museums. It may take effort on your part to stimulate and encourage your child in her areas of interest. If you're not sure what interests your child, expose her to lots of ideas and topics, and consider comments she makes.

At home, it helps to stock your shelves with interesting learning resources to stimulate your child's imagination and help create a desire for learning. Make these shelves easily accessible to your child and fill them with games, puzzles, magazines, books, art supplies, and classical music tapes. Use them often, *with* your child, to open his mind to possibilities.

Use mealtimes to teach as spontaneous questions arise. If you keep a globe or atlas near the dinner table, you can grab it in a split second when talk of world or U.S. events pops up. If your child receives a letter from a cousin and wants to know where the cousin lives, she might look under her plate—at her placemat with a map of the United States! Or if she asks the location of a country she has heard about in school, church, or on the news, you can grab your globe and spin to that country on the spot. You will find your children absorbing and remembering geography information with little effort on your part to "teach" them.

LEARNING DIFFERENCES.

Children have many different learning styles and learn at different rates. Some of this is related to personality. Author and speaker

Cynthia Tobias, mother of identical twins, says even they have different learning styles. Even our genetic blueprint cannot fully explain the mystery of individuality!

Personality also affects how interested children are in language skills. Some have an inborn love for language and may eventually become speakers, writers, or teachers and be voracious readers. Other children are more fascinated by how things are organized, be that words, math, or science concepts. They may use words functionally and skillfully, but they may not end up reading for the pure pleasure of it.

Some, like my son and Cassie's daughter, Meg, are eager, almost insatiable learners—a true joy to teach. I must admit that can bring out the best in a mother who initially lacks confidence in her ability to teach. Remember my swing phonics game with Tyler? He was two and a half at the time—and was making the "two sticks with a line" *H*'s at age three. He has continued to learn at an accelerated rate, with a combination of home-schooling, international schooling, and gifted education in the public schools. As for Meg, I recall asking her, when she was tiny, how old she was, expecting her to hold up two fingers. When she replied, "Twenty-one months. I'll be two in November," I about fell on the floor! It's easy to see why Cassie was particularly discouraged when she was unable to play much with Meg during the first year of colicky Luke's life. It had become personally rewarding to her to teach her child. The good news is that Luke is now well and a joy to teach as well—though he learns differently from his sister.

Some children with organized minds and excellent memories yearn to make sense of language symbols early on. In Tyler's case, he wanted to begin using them in practical ways—for instance, to write wish lists for Christmas or a list of chores. But other children may be attracted to language for other reasons. Aimee has a natural attraction to reading and writing as I do, with a strong desire to communicate feelings and creativity.

Then there are the Elisas in this world who are more intrigued by the ways their bodies work, and in improving physical skills, than they are in the printed page. Elisa is learning to read at a normal rate, but she will trade a pen for roller skates or a basketball any day.

And some children truly struggle when it comes to grasping language symbols and sounds. I'll have to delve into that more in a different book, yet I do want to acknowledge the difficulties this can cause when parents and children play together. Children with learning disabilities usually possess average to above-average intelligence—they can even be intellectually gifted. Yet there's no denying that activities requiring the use of language skills can be frustrating and can lead to feelings of helplessness in a parent. It can be a challenge to meet a child's educational needs (which may steal time from play) or enjoy parent-child play when common childhood games aren't easily comprehended.

One mom has a son who struggles in this area. He's now sixteen. They enjoy playing dice or card games together, but games like Catch Phrase or Scrabble are far more difficult. It pains this mother when she sees her son try to play games with other teens, yet he can't make out the vowel sounds on a game card he must read aloud. She wonders if it might have been better for her to spend more time playing games with him that would have given him more practice in areas where he struggled, despite his frustration. Or maybe it was good to reserve playtimes to focus on his strengths, instead. Perhaps families like this need a little of both kinds of play. If you have a child who struggles with language who is getting special education help, I suggest you ask his therapists how you can best help your child through play.

5 minute fun

WHAT SWIMS? WHAT FLIES?

Choose a category. Alternate naming items in that category until one of you has brain freeze. For example, "swimmers" can range from sharks to submarines, "fliers" can be anything from hot-air balloons to eagles. Don't be surprised if your three-year-old beats you.

WHAT AM I?

Ask your child to be an animal and make you guess which one. Tell him how to give you clues about color, size, etc. and to pantomime how the animal acts.

> "I'm gray, with big ears and a tiny tail. What am I?"
> "A mouse!"
> "No, bigger, and I walk around like this . . ."
> "An elephant!"

time to get out! or stay in?

Using Local Resources, from Museums to Moms' Groups

So much to do and so many places to see. Is it time to stay home, to replace too much busyness with simple cuddles? Or do you long to get out? to connect with other parents and kids and boost your enthusiasm for parenting?

Whew. In a single month, we had dashed from one kid-pleasing activity to another. We treated our two-and-a-half-year-old to the Discovery Point Zoo (where he liked the animals but loved the water fountain). Next we drove to the Olympic Game Farm, where he got "slurped" when a "buffalope" stuck his enormous tongue in our window. Then we drove to the "hot dog" (hot springs) and finally the circus. Hey, it was summer vacation!

After settling back in at home, I asked him, "Tyler, what was your favorite thing we did this last month?" I was confident that he would gleefully describe one of our recent adventures.

He thought carefully, then replied, "Layin' on Mom and layin' on Dad." I smiled, thinking of all the times since Tyler was a tiny baby when he'd lain contentedly on the rising and falling chest of his daddy (even when Dad was snoring loudly, with a remote control falling from his hand). And I thought of our Roly-Poly game, with me as the human amusement ride. I would lie on the floor and roll wildly from side to side with Tyler as he giggled and clutched me tightly so he wouldn't fall off. That need for touch is so often unmet when we are racing around in cars.

His second favorite? "You or Dad layin' on my floor, watchin' me do a puzzle or make a tower with my blocks." Hmm. It's hard to cheer for a kid—to even *see* him—when he's strapped in the backseat and Mom and Dad are in the front seat, watching the road or map reading.

Oh, the money, time, and energy we could have saved! Yes, Tyler definitely enjoyed our outings, as evidenced by his repeatedly telling others about the slurping buffalope. But what he liked best were cuddles and concentrated attention.

Activities designed for family togetherness can actually interfere with it sometimes. In our household, the time I'm least likely to give my kids any one-on-one attention is when we are preparing for a trip. Pretrip stress always throws me into a tizzy: Should I pack the liquid Tylenol (just in case)? Let's see . . . we need three pairs of Mickey Mouse underwear, and where is that kiddie audiotape? Always, during my frantic packing (as if on cue), Tyler would hang on my leg and whine, "Let's play, Mommy."

"Not now, honey! Now hurry and get your coat on, use the bathroom, and . . ."

"But I don't have to go!"

"We always go potty before a long car ride, Sweetheart. Now after you do that, then hop in the car . . ."

"But I wanna stay home!"

"We're going so you can have *fun!* Now *get in that car!*"

Sometimes we are so busy preparing for a trip that we forget to take time to explain to the kids what we are doing and why we are doing it. We forget that a preschooler's sense of time is different from our own, and we may need to explain that the car ride will be about as long as his favorite TV show or movie. A small child simply can't fathom why we would make him use the potty when he doesn't have to go.

It's easy to forget to look at fun from the kid's point of view. To a child, wrestling on the carpet now may be much more appealing than getting straitjacketed into a car seat to enjoy the zoo later. Not that we shouldn't take trips to the zoo—they make for fond family memories. We simply need to find a balance between time away and time at home.

When I am busiest, I can't even look at the local parenting newspapers with their calendars full of things to see and places to go. After moving from a rural area offering so little to an urban area offering an overwhelming abundance, I often feel guilty for not taking my kids to things I know they would enjoy.

Yet I feel much compassion for families who can't sit down together for dinner very often because their kids are all engaged in different activities.

Reflect back on the chapter on time and energy barriers to see if you can cut down on any unnecessary activities—even those that are child related. When was the last time you all just slumped around the living room together and watched a movie?

Our family often used to have "movie nights," complete with a dinner eaten on a sheet spread on the living-room floor, picnic style. Dinner consisted of Ritz crackers with lunch meats and cheeses, fruits, a veggie tray with dip, and, of course, popcorn. We had a hide-a-bed in our living-room couch. When Tyler and Aimee were small, we'd flip that out and pile it high with pillows. Then we'd all snuggle to watch the movie in the dark, theater style. Now that the kids are bigger it's harder to fit everyone—and to find movies that please everyone—but on occasion it still works. The key was in making it an event—a big production, a date for all. (In other words, no popping in the movie while Mom or Dad does dishes!)

As your children grow, and their own schedules get more and more hectic and separate from your own, it will take some creativity and planning to get everyone together to relax at home, all in the same room. But your family does need some quiet time together.

TIME TO GET OUT!

On the flip side, perhaps you're feeling isolated at home all day with several small children. Are you feeling as if you've been stuck in the house for far too long? Staying inside day after day, with no contact with other adults and no change of scenery, can indeed be depressing. Just after you change out of the sweatshirt with spit-up on the shoulder, your fresh shirt may be instantly covered with little peanut-butter-and-jelly handprints. This is enough to cause any mom to lose heart. Who cares? Who's going to see you anyway? That's when you know it's time for a change of pace.

However, you may not know what kinds of things there are to do with your kids in your area. Or maybe you feel shy about venturing out. One mom shared that she found it difficult to find other stay-at-home moms in her city and she was looking foward to her daughter starting kindergarten just so she could get acquainted with other mothers.

Another parent said she found it tough to handle the logistics of getting out with four kids under age seven. Yet even two kids can be a handful when they're misbehaving! The effort to get out may seem overwhelming. Pack the diaper bag. Time the outing perfectly between naps. And it can be so annoying to constantly buckle and unbuckle car seats—if you even have a car to drive. And if you are at the bottom of a downward spiral, depression can keep you from taking any action at all.

Please don't feel defeated! Be honest: Can you sort out legitimate reasons from excuses? Have you truly made an effort to find other parents in your area? Do you have any options for transportation besides driving? Have you explored what there is to do in your area? Can your children help more when you all want to go out?

You don't have to be isolated! If you have been inside for a long time, getting out to do the simplest things may seem more difficult than it really is. It certainly won't be easy, but it may be just what you need to get an emotional lift and some interesting fruit for conversations with your kids. I've had a lot of funny and fascinating talks with my children about places we've been, especially because I always take a lot of photos to rekindle our memories later. That goes for even brief little jaunts to the park. Also, the more often you get out, the easier it becomes.

Let's look at four issues: finding fun places to go, coordinating it with kids, getting there, and finding companionship.

FINDING FUN PLACES TO GO

Even in the smallest of towns, you can find things to do and people to meet through the following places:

Libraries. These often have story times for preschoolers (you can usually take your baby, too) as well as other, more elaborate programs—for instance, jugglers or even live parrots! Even small-town libraries are usually connected to a larger system that sponsors traveling programs. Bookstores also have reading times.

Parent play groups. Some groups are sponsored by hospitals. Other groups for parents of young children are national or international. (See sidebar on pages 186–187.) Quite often parents who meet at such groups form friendships that endure for many years. In one Moms in Touch group, several of the women have been meeting since their children, now in high school, were in early elementary school.

Fast-food joints with play areas. Check your phone book or ask other parents in the area for recommendations. This is a great way to get out of the house yet stay in an enclosed, safe environment.

City parks and recreation departments. There are often indoor playgrounds held in community centers a few times a week; call and ask. These are normally designed for children from about one to four years old. They are held in gyms and contain inflatable or plastic play equipment, mats, balls, trikes and child-sized cars, play kitchens, etc. You can rest on the sidelines or get in and play, too. You can also sign up for parent-child classes on topics from dance to science.

Local schools. A good way to introduce little ones to the theater is to take them to public-school productions. When Aimee was in *The Wizard of Oz*, Elisa was excited to watch her sister, but she also insisted I take photos of her with every actor afterwards. The high school–aged Dorothy blushed a little at that, but to Elisa it was just as grand as getting a photo with a Disneyland character.

Your local Chamber of Commerce or Tourist Information Center, city newspaper, and local parenting newspapers all may have information about special events and ongoing exhibits. Don't forget to see if there are any nearby. Some examples:

Amusement parks
Zoos and aquariums
Museums of art, flight, or history
Hands-on museums just for kids
Factory tours (candy, automobile, cheese, etc.)
Craft and/or vegetable markets
U-pick fruit fields
Caverns, lakes, interesting bike trails, or other natural wonders

COORDINATING IT WITH KIDS

Now that you have an idea of a few places to go, let's talk about the logistics of getting out the door. By making some activities routine, you'll be able to do that more quickly. It helps when the kids come to expect what a certain kind of activity will be like and they know how to behave when they get there. For instance, you might go to the library's preschool story hour every Wednesday at 10:00, or play at the McDonald's area or a park every Tuesday, or dress up for church every Sunday. My friend Cassie says that doing the latter

MOTHERS' SUPPORT GROUPS

MOPS (Mothers of Preschoolers www.mops.org). This encouraging faith-based support organization for parents has groups meeting in over two thousand locations in the U.S. and in nineteen countries. From ten to two hundred moms meet every few weeks or monthly for mentoring, parenting instruction (sometimes from guest speakers), and creative activities, while children are cared for in a preschool-like setting. You can find a MOPS group in your area by typing in your zip code on their Web site. You may find similar groups under different names, for instance Moms and Moppets, which are not affiliated with MOPS but have similar programs and goals.

MOMS Clubs (Mothers Offering Mothers Support www.momsclub.com). This is a nonpro helped her keep her sanity even when she was exhausted from her baby's colic. Putting on a dress and makeup, getting to be with other adults, and hearing uplifting music was quite healing for her.

Instead of, or in addition to, weekly outings, you might have seasonal ones and make a bigger effort to drive just a little farther than usual (or take a bus with your kids), say to a field of tulips to photograph your child. Or you can take your little ones to a blueberry patch. Blueberries are easy to pick and don't stain little hands; blackberries can be poky and messy, but they're still fun to eat. Let the kids help you make a pie when you get home—even if you use a premade frozen pie shell.

Community events like Easter egg hunts can be fun to look forward to. In our town there's a bike, tricycle, and stroller parade. Kids dress up in costumes and decorate their bikes with streamers. At the end of the parade each child gets two dollars for participating.

Getting bigger kids out for educational purposes is great for the whole family or for groups of children, especially if you are homeschooling. When we lived about three hours away from the Seattle area, we were part of a homeschool group. Many of the fourth graders in that group were learning how to read charts and schedules. It seemed quite silly to learn those skills out of a math book, so I led the group on a one-day field trip to Seattle.

We carpooled up the east side of the Olympic Peninsula then boarded ferries to Seattle. Once in the city, we took the bus to Pioneer Square, then the monorail to the Seattle Center. Then we did

ligious group with over 1,500 chapters. Activities vary from club to club but may include field trips to zoos and parks; reading times at bookstores; MOMS nights out; activity groups (for instance, scrapbooking or walking); and baby-sitting co-ops.

MITI (Moms in Touch International www.momsintouch.org) is a more specialized national support group designed for mothers to connect to pray for each other's children. MITI groups meet in individual homes (sometimes alternating homes) once every week or two for an hour. You can e-mail the organization through their Web site. They will search to see if there is an existing group through your child's public or private school, or if there is one for homeschoolers in your area.

it all in reverse; in all, we deciphered about six schedules. Even the adults, many of whom had never been to Seattle, were shocked at what we had accomplished in a single day.

I admit that trip required a lot of gumption. Our destination that day is now just a hop, skip, and a jump from where I live, but I constantly make excuses not to go since traffic intimidates me. But we can get there with a few bus transfers! I also tend to get into the "been there, done that" mode. But when reviewing old photos, I sometimes realize that only a first child experienced an outing—five years ago—and the younger kids never have. Come to think of it, Elisa has never been blueberry picking . . . yet!

No, it's not always easy to get out. Buses are late, kids throw public tantrums, babies fall asleep or cry at inconvenient times. . . . But it's worth the effort. And the more you get out, the more your kids will help you do what it takes to get out. Elisa is enormously independent; this once led to a funny incident with her dad. He was planning to take her out somewhere, but he didn't realize that when *I* say, "Let's go," she's often, within minutes, not only dressed and packed but has climbed into the car and buckled her own car seat.

On this particular day, Dad said, "Let's go" but proceeded to piddle around for a while, making himself coffee. He then found Elisa in the car already. Her comment was particularly funny, considering her penchant for lifting lines out of movies and mimicking the actor's voices, then inserting them appropriately into situations. She complained, "Dad, I've been waiting so long for you." Then she twisted her mouth sideways and (copying the Grinch, who in the movie panicked when his sled went out of control) said, "I almost lost my cool there!"

GETTING THERE

No car? How about just getting out of the house for a walk every day the sun is shining? If you do it often enough, your kids will know exactly what to expect and how to behave. It can be frightening if kids are impulsive and tend to run toward traffic, so you must train them not to. With toddlers, my rule was: "You *must* sit in the stroller or wear the hand-holder. You choose." (The hand-holder was a stretchy cord that on one end attached with Velcro to the back of my child's overalls and on the other attached to the stroller or the purse on my shoulder.) Preschoolers may run ahead a half-block on the sidewalk, but they must stop *immediately* when you shout, "Stop!" Practice playing red light, green light. Kids love walks. If they disobey, go home immediately, even if *you* want to stay out. Give them another chance later, reinforcing that obedience is a must for you to have fun, worry-free walks.

One of the best investments I ever made was a huge jogging stroller. I used it for ten years. Two plastic molded bike seats on it enabled me to take very long walks with babies or even tired preschoolers. Even loaded to the gills, with its twenty-four-inch bicycle tires, the thing moved with the flip of a finger. I could push two forty-pound kids and two grocery bags with one hand, and walk while holding a latte with the other. What a machine! We even walked on ferries for overnighters to Canada and within Norway by piling the stroller high with luggage. We hiked on mountain trails with it bouncing over tree roots, and we pushed it through snow.

However, I put the most mileage on it when we lived in a small town. A one-mile walk to the bank, post office, and grocery store gave us our exercise and mail in one fell swoop. When we moved to a more urban area with mail delivery, we had to find other excuses to get out and walk. I'd get out a map and pick *any* destination within a mile that might give us a reward: the convenience store for Slurpees, the library for story hour, or Daddy's office to meet him for lunch. Often we'd take the bus back home. Buses will accommodate big strollers just as they do wheelchairs; they can even lower the electric platform for you *(beep . . . beep . . . beep)*, which toddlers find exciting.

I almost put a bumper sticker on the stroller declaring, "My other car is a station wagon."

Older kids can walk instead of riding, and you might be astonished at how far they can go with the proper motivation. Our four-year-old walked about five miles one week—between walks downtown from our residential area and a weekend hike with Dad. Some kids whine more than others on walks, but the more you get out, the more endurance they'll build. They can use their trikes or bikes while you walk.

Your child may lose steam while walking or triking and insist that you carry him or his bike. Ask him to race you or chase you—to run, not walk! I know it's bizarre, but it has worked with all three of my kids—getting up to another half-mile out of them to get home or to where the car is parked.

FINDING COMPANIONSHIP

One day in Norway, I was working in the kitchen when five-year-old Aimee came running in, panting, "Mom! Mom! There's a neighbor out working in her yard we haven't met yet!"

I had the ultimate excuse to be isolated when I was home full-time, pregnant, and few of my neighbors spoke English. Also, Norwegians have a reputation for being rather shy. It became obvious that I would have to make some first moves if I wanted to find some friends.

And so Aimee and I became quite bold, not only approaching neighbors in their yards to say hello but once even walking right up to a house with a stroller on the porch to introduce myself with my five-year-old. Many of the women I met were as isolated as I was and were grateful for our visit, inviting us in for coffee; some became long-term friends.

The thought of approaching strangers may scare you half to death if you're shy by nature. It does get easier the more you try it. For instance, as you push your child on a swing while another mother pushes hers, you can ask casual questions: "How long have you lived in the area?" or "Have you found any fun places to go with your kids that you can recommend?"

It may be just as difficult for you to engage in conversations in groups—even those specifically designed for parents to get together. Just remember that others are probably there for the same reason you are—companionship and a change of pace. Never assume that the person next to you has been going there forever and knows everyone else already. And if they have or do, they will probably want to meet you, too! You're probably not the only one who wants to share bottom-wiping woes or teenage trials.

Parents usually have great compassion for one another and may even be delighted to offer practical help like giving you and your kids rides to meetings or swapping play dates. Then again, you may end up being the one who gives to others just what they need.

I had one friendship that I always thought was very one sided. I met Elin in Norway. Our daughters were in preschool together, and from the moment we met, she insisted on helping me whenever I needed it—watching baby Elisa so I could go to Norwegian language classes and keeping my kids for me when Gordy was hospitalized. One morning when I had the flu and could not move a muscle, she was there in ten minutes flat. It actually embarrassed me a little. I felt at that time that I was so needy and had so little to give back.

But when I had to move away, she cried. She said she had never before met anyone with whom she could pray on the spur of the moment. About what? Oh, parent concerns—for instance the anger she sometimes felt with her children. She felt unattractive and unaccomplished. But her warmth, her smile, her sense of humor delighted me, and I was in awe of her ability to speak four different languages. I had connected her with other mothers whom I knew would enjoy her and she them.

Don't underestimate the power you have to encourage others simply by being willing to let others encourage you.

START SOMETHING NEW

If there isn't an established group in your area, you might consider starting one. If you have a child registered for kindergarten in the fall, why wait until then to meet the other kids' families? Ask the principal if you can organize a potluck at the park so the kids can begin getting to know each other before school begins. That can make the start of school easier for everyone.

When Tyler was in fifth grade, we moved to a new town in the middle of the school year. We visited the school on a Thursday, but the principal said to wait until Monday to start. The next day, three children appeared at the door asking to meet Tyler; the principal had told them about the new kid on the block. The kids played all weekend, and by Monday Tyler started school with new friends! Wow. If kids can be bold enough to do that, why can't we?

Sometimes it takes extra effort to connect with other families. Large churches often sponsor small groups for families, singles, moms, or dads to meet for mutual encouragement. We looked into a few but none in our area were for whole families—and we wanted our kids to make some new friends. We decided to start our own family group, we got some leadership training, and we put an ad in the church bulletin. The result? We connected with about ten families! The youngest in one family, Alexandra, became Elisa's best friend—and her mom and I have been trading child care once a week now for about two years. On the days I have both Alex and Elisa, I try to take time to play, but in exchange I have another morning off to myself.

Other mothers have started their own chapters of the moms' groups I mention in the sidebar, learning or enhancing leadership skills in the process. Some groups form their own baby-sitting co-ops as well as enjoying time as a group.

Is it time to stay in with your kids, to hibernate for a while, to regain some intimacy? Cut back on activities and enjoy some downtime together as a family.

Or has it been far too long since you've gotten out? Throw your kids in the car and head for the nearest U-pick berry field or museum. Or start planning an even greater adventure—your next family vacation!

BEAR HUNT

Give a tot or two a flashlight, and at dusk, go on a backyard bear hunt. Chant the bear-hunt rhyme while letting the kids search for stuffed bears you've tucked among the bushes! You can even cut out bear paw prints and laminate them to use over and over again out in the yard. (*Contributed by Joanne Reidt.*)

SHADOW STOMP

When you're out on a walk together or your preschooler is riding his trike as you walk, he may lose steam before you can get back home. Boost his motivation and energy by saying, "Don't you *dare* run over my shadow!"

When he does (of course!), scream in agony or moan.

An alternative is to play shadow tag. Try stomping on each other's shadows before you can run to a place where your shadows are hidden in the shade of a tree or a car.

INVISIBLE FRUIT

Take turns peeling and eating invisible fruit while the other person guesses what kind it is. (Or you can just let your child do this while you rest and guess.) We have played this game at countless birthday parties—even with children who spoke no English! (There's only one way to peel a banana!)

chapter 14

Family Adventures

Are you ready to roam farther now? to leave your

neighborhood, your city, your state—even your

country? Let's take a look at how much

fun family vacations can be!

One mother told Gordy and me that she and her husband always vacationed without their kids. "Family vacations never worked out," she said. Gordy and I felt quite sorry for her, and even a bit horrified. For us, the word *vacation* is synonymous with *family time.*

Not that I don't enjoy a mini-escape once in a while—a weekend away with my husband or some alone time at a ladies' retreat. It's nice occasionally to be responsible for no one but myself. But the word *vacation* gives Gordy and me instant flashbacks to funny and fascinating family times, which often had less to do with where we were than with what our children said or did. Vacations without our children are fuzzy memories. Vacation memories *with* our kids, however, have created vivid snapshots and minivideos in our minds, as well as on film. We've captured great images of our kids at ages and stages they have too quickly grown out of. Here's a sampling:

- Four-year-old Aimee, in a tropical paradise, is riding in a taxi with us on a winding road, overlooking a small village. She suddenly and mysteriously shrieks in terror, "Aaagh!" and covers her eyes. Alarmed, we ask, "What's wrong?" "I hate pink houses!" she replies, eyes wide.

⑨ The whole Sargent crew plummets down a waterfall, screaming in unison as we grip the safety bars. When the ride stops, we run like mad to get in line to do it all over again.

⑨ Preschooler Elisa asks to be buried in the sand, all but her head. Suddenly Gordy, Tyler, and Aimee get a wild idea. They sculpt in the sand, below Elisa's tiny grinning face, the body of a six-foot-tall muscle man. I take the picture an instant before she absolutely *must* scratch her nose and sits up, crumbling her bulging biceps.

⑨ Teenage Tyler points his laser pen into the dark around our campsite and causes the red speck to dance from tree to tree. He raises the pitch of his voice to talk in his "bitin' bee" squeaky voice to three-year-old Elisa, who follows the bee and talks back quite seriously to it. Later, as they hike through lush woods with surprise waterfalls, big brother reaches down and puts little sis on his shoulders to help her make it to the end of the trail.

Frankly, I can hardly write this without yearning to get away with the kids somewhere. We always look forward to that week or two when we can escape work worries and household hassles to focus on each other and the kids. It almost doesn't matter where we go.

Not that it's always a breeze. What do you think might "not work" on a family trip? Loads of things. You might argue about when to go, or where to go, or how to get there, or when to stop and rest. You might have very different ideas about what is fun. However, with some creative thinking, you can often find ways for everyone to have some of what they consider fun. And you may well discover that as you travel, the most memorable and fun moments end up being those that occur simply from being together.

Does the idea of traveling afar excite you or intimidate you? Perhaps both? If your family is anything like ours, your list of places may be long and alluring. There aren't enough days in a lifetime to see all we'd like to see. Perhaps my husband and I enjoy traveling so much because we grew up in families that traveled. As a child, I saw many sights, including national parks, en route to a new home, because my dad worked for the U.S. Forest Service and we lived in five different states over the course of my childhood. Moving allowed us to see the great diversity in our country.

I have vague memories of me and my brothers tussling in the backseat and whining about who got the window next, while our parents insisted through gritted teeth, "Look at the beautiful scenery!" Yet my siblings and I grew up wanting to take *our* kids to see such magnificent sights too.

Does travel naturally intrigue you, or are you more of a home-body? If you didn't travel much as a child, leaving the comforts of home may intimidate you a little. You may even worry, *What if things go wrong?* Well, on occasion they do. But mishaps can make for colorful family lore! And the odds are, the more your family travels together and learns to work together as a team, the more fond memories will override less pleasant ones. I urge you to avoid letting what-ifs prevent you from venturing out.

CONQUERING VACATION PROCRASTINATION

Let's take a look at all that goes into planning a family vacation:

- Deciding where to go and how to get there
- Finding time off, from school and work, for the whole family
- Paying for it
- Keeping it stress free and uncomplicated
- Knowing what kind of travel will fit your children's ages and personalities
- Getting along with each other once you're on the road (or wing, or waves), or better yet, having a blast together

Where to Go
Vacations are generally designed with a goal in mind. You may want to get to a different climate—to swim and snorkel, or to ski and sled. Or you may want to see a different type of topography. It

can be exciting to go from a flat, dry desert to a lush, mossy rain forest—or vice versa. You may even want to see another culture and hear foreign languages and music—even if that means simply crossing the border into Mexico.

Then again, you may be more entertained by modern marvels: technology or thrill rides, like those at Disneyland or Six Flags. Or your goal may be as simple as getting away from home, anywhere at all, just to get the whole family out of the house and the kids away from their peers.

If you're like us, you may want to do all of these things. Seeing extended family in other states is often a driving force for us as we consider where to go and what to do. However, we always manage to see fascinating sites along the way. On our last trip to Georgia to see the grandparents, a side trip took us to an underground cavern with stalactites and stalagmites.

The Internet is a fabulous resource for finding places to go. Look at travel books as well; they've got great ideas.

Time and Money

Getting time off together can be tricky, especially as the children get older and their school schedules get busier. It takes some long-range planning with everyone's calendars to make trips happen. I'm already looking at vacations a year from now (at least a general time frame and potential destination).

You may need to budget far ahead for money as well as time. If you have any disposable income at all, then spending some of it on family travel is largely a matter of choice. That may mean sacrifice. We've been able to take some great trips partly because we've never purchased a new car. (The memories from family vacations last much longer than that new-car smell!) We pinch pennies in other ways too, especially when we have a particular trip in mind. The kids have small clothing budgets and we eat out less. We usually pay our credit cards off every month to avoid wasting money on interest. Yet every single credit-card purchase earns us airline mileage.

That's actually been a key to financing our biggest family vacations—accumulating airline mileage for years until we have enough to go somewhere exotic. For about five years, we accumulated miles for our whole family. We then looked at the globe to find the farthest place we could fly with that mileage: St. Thomas, in the Virgin Islands. It was there that Aimee startled us with her pink-house horror. We also fondly recall her repeatedly exclaiming in her high voice, as she saw countless lizards, "It's just like a *zoo* here!" We have some amazing photographs of her feeding bright red hibiscus flowers to an iguana that was as long as Aimee was tall. Tyler was harder to photograph. For most of that trip, all we saw of him was his flippers sticking out of the water as he snorkeled.

We're now on round two, having accumulated miles again for another five years. We have to go somewhere soon, to use (or else lose) those miles; that's a great motivator for family vacations.

You can also save money by trying different modes of travel. As our family has grown, it has gotten more expensive to fly to see family. Train fares tend to cost about the same as plane fares. However, Amtrak once ran a special through coupons at a local pizza place, enabling our entire family to choo-choo from the Northwest to southern California for only $400. It was a long, long ride, but we saved a bundle.

There are also some interesting ways to save money on the road. I discovered, by accident, a great money saver on hotel rooms. Once, on a road trip through eastern Washington, with no air conditioning in the car, we became desperate for a hotel room with a swimming pool. I bargained with a hotel manager for a better price—and got it. We paid fifty dollars for a room instead of eighty.

Lo and behold, I have discovered that room rates even at the finest hotels can be negotiable. You're most likely to be successful after 6:00 P.M., when hotels often get cancellations, and during off-season. If there is any chance the rooms might not be filled on a particular night—for which the management must still pay heat or air conditioning—the desk clerk or manager is probably willing to negotiate. You must be subtle. Don't ask loudly when there is a crowd in the lobby. It amuses me what often happens when I'm quoted a rate and I simply ask politely, "Can I get a better rate than that?" The person at the desk writes a new price on a Post-it note and hands it to me. Often they'll ask if you qualify for one of their lower rates with AAA or some such thing. If the answer is no, ask if you can fill out a survey for them or some such thing to get the special rate; they often don't need much of an excuse to give it to you.

We tried this at a very fancy hotel once, and the desk clerk actually looked apologetic. He said he was sorry, but there was a conference in town so he had to fill every room at full price that particular night—but to feel free to ask in the future. It takes guts to ask for a lower rate or free breakfast. But do try asking anytime you think that a hotel may not be full for the night. The worst they can do is say no.

Less Stress

One type of getaway our family enjoys is camping and hiking. However, I must admit that I'm not your conventional camper. Many camping parents enjoy packing every conceivable bit of gear and food necessary to cook in the woods. Frankly, that's not my cup of campfire cocoa. Packing and unpacking for camping trips is something I actually detest. I also don't really enjoy getting too dirty, cooking outdoors, or doing dishes on vacation.

Our "camping" vacation to Yellowstone National Park was a fabulous experience for our entire family. Gordy is a more enthusiastic camper than I am, so I'm grateful that he was agreeable to alternating nights between campsites and hotels with swimming pools. On vacations like this, we usually eat one meal per day at a restaurant and pack snack foods, grocery deli items, and fruit for the other meals. The only meal I recall cooking on our weeklong Jellystone—oops—*Yellowstone* trip was hot dogs and Jiffy Pop— the popcorn that's more fun to cook over the campfire than it is to eat. (By the way, the kids were disappointed that we saw no Yogis or BooBoo bears.) Oh, and of course s'mores are a requirement— heavy on the chocolate, please.

We also managed to get by with very little camping gear. We have a nice tent, but we have yet to buy sleeping bags for everyone in the family. I have discovered that a few down comforters from our beds roll up tighter and keep us just as warm, and with a decent pad or inflatable mattress we do fine.

Sometimes you can get back to nature in a single, yet fantastic, day trip. One June, we hiked as a family to a gorgeous lake in the Mount Baker, Washington, area. The Forest Service calls it "Lake 22."

I must admit I'm not in the best hiking shape. What got me up the winding, rocky, muddy, 2.7 miles was the vision of the cheese-cake I'd enjoyed the week before melting off my thighs (one piece for each leg). Some incredible visual rewards along the way helped as well: cedar trees eight feet across, a roaring waterfall, lush green ferns. As we hiked, Elisa and I had a mini–spiritual discussion about how our faith could ground us and hold us up much like massive roots held up those towering cedars. I photographed Aimee against the scenery, startled by the beauty of both. I was grateful that Tyler was cheerfully with us on a day he could so easily have been hangin' with his buds in town. Instead, there he was, encouraging his sib-lings to race ahead with him as Gordy and I panted behind.

After navigating the last half-mile on hard-packed snow, we rounded a bend in the trail and an opening in the trees, and . . . wow. Rising up from the opposite shore of the small lake was a majestic, snow-capped mountain, with small waterfalls making tracks like tears through lush green trees. We sat in the sun on a small dam of logs, stunned, trying to think of a name for that place that was far more majestic than its current name. Even Sargent Lake would be better than Lake 22! When we realized it was getting a bit nippy and our stomachs were growling, we began our downward trek. I was grateful for gravity and began salivating at the thought of leftover cheesecake in the fridge at home. Hey, I deserved it, right? Elisa and I kept our feet moving by singing "The Bear Went over the Mountain," a varia-tion from our usual "The Ants Go Marching One by One."

When we arrived home, we realized that in only one short day, we had really squeezed in a minivacation.

Great Expectations

Of course, bigger trips take more thought, and successful ones should take into consideration your children's ages, interests, and abilities. Nevertheless, I hope you won't underestimate your kids. One common mistake is to assume that a trip you have in mind will only work when your children reach a certain age.

Of course, there is some wisdom in considering this. Taking a toddler—who can run but not yet reason well—to see Notre Dame will quickly turn you into an exhausted hunchback. I would certainly never have planned to take a ten-month-old baby in a stroller, a six-year-old, and an eleven-year-old to Notre Dame. After all, I thought, they were surely too young to appreciate it, and besides, we could never afford it. Then suddenly, serendipitously, we had the opportunity to go to Europe. Impulsively, we went.

I'd like to share a little about that trip with you, because while the scenery and architecture were certainly glorious, more glorious were the lessons we learned about successfully and joyfully traveling as a family. Even if it's unlikely you will see Europe yourself, I hope what we learned might encourage you. You see, we discovered a few keys to enjoying our time together, which we've found can be applied to traveling anywhere as a family—from a simple camping trip a few hours from home to a flight to see Grandma and Grandpa.

What were those keys? Spontaneity, flexibility, and simplicity . . . with playfulness and trust thrown in for good measure.

RAILROAD TIES

"Run! Run!" we cried out to each other. "We're going to make it!"

Our little family *flew* up the long flight of stairs to the next train platform. Gordy raced ahead with a soft suitcase in each hand and a duffel on his back. He slowed a bit to encourage Aimee, who stumbled as she adjusted her backpack. Tyler and I followed, Tyler reaching behind him to hold the front of sister Elisa's umbrella stroller as I ran behind holding up the back. As we bump-bumped along crazily, Elisa grinned a two-toothed grin, clutching the sides of her ride.

We all darted through the train's open doors, then plopped into our seats, sweaty yet jubilant. "Three minutes to spare!" Tyler cried out. We cheered.

Whew. The exhilaration! The *what?* Sounds like stress to you?

Perhaps. But by a week into our trip, we had become seasoned train travelers. Oh, we had a few glitches, but we had learned to work efficiently as a family. In addition to discovering how we were able to work together to reach a common goal—like catching a train on time—we also discovered what capable people our children were.

Believe it or not, that day (and most other days on that trip) we had no room reservations for the night, although we did have destination cities. We weren't even sure what sites we would see, other than a few key places, such as the Eiffel Tower. That may cause those of you who love to plan all the details of trips in advance to shudder.

Much of the spontaneity of that trip was forced on us. We could so easily have been locked into complex plans—a natural thing to do when planning a trip of such magnitude. However, the problem (or blessing in disguise) was that we had no time to plan the trip before we actually went. We were in the midst of preparing to move back to the United States from Norway, where we had lived for nearly two years. In the middle of packing, closing out bank accounts, and selling our house, we suddenly realized that unless we saw Europe while we were still on that side of the Atlantic, we might never have another chance.

So with only a few weeks to go, and no spare minutes to actually *plan* our trip, we paid in advance for Eurail tickets for a ten-day trip. That would allow us to ride the rails through any of seventeen different countries, getting on and off whenever and wherever we pleased. We thought we would shoot for five countries. But we had no idea what we'd be able to realistically see with three small children. What in the world was in store for us? Much of my life up to this point had revolved around elementary-school soccer games, diaper changes, shopping for sack lunches, and washing dirty socks.

Although I consider myself fairly footloose, that trip was *so* loosely planned it made even me a little nervous. Our only hotel reservations were in Amsterdam—"bookending" the train trip—to ensure we had a place to stay the first night and the last, just before we had to fly back to the United States. We had no idea how long it would take to get from one country to another. We did not know how tiring it would be, what we should try to see, or for how long!

It wasn't quite as risky as it sounds, however. September was off-season, and our guidebook assured us there would be plenty of open hotel rooms wherever we went (there were). The book also suggested one strategy that looked promising. We would try to arrive in our targeted cities by early afternoon, go straight to the visitor's bureaus, and get help finding hotels. We would figure out sites to see by reading our guidebook on the train itself. (This strategy worked!)

One element to our traveling successfully, the *best* decision of the entire trip, was traveling as lightly as possible. How lightly? You may not believe this, but for the trains, we whittled down our luggage to whatever we knew we could literally run with. It actually made the difference between our making or not making connections. We also felt less tired because we had less to carry, and we were less stressed with fewer bags to count.

You see, our trial run from the airport to the hotel in Amsterdam had overwhelmed us at the start. Remember that we were in the process of moving. We were carrying six weeks' worth of goods, since our kids were to start school in the U.S. a month before our moving container would arrive on a ship from Norway. We had an unbelievable amount of stuff, two-thirds of which we were graciously allowed to store at the Amsterdam hotel for a week.

Then we each took one small, plastic grocery bag to fit our clothes in for the train trip! For most of us, that meant only one or two spares of every item of clothing. Elisa got the most variety with her microscopic clothes, which all fit in a Ziploc bag. We fit clothes for our entire family in two carry-on-sized suitcases. Do I hear clapping, or cries of disbelief? Hey, I can *still* fill a bag that size with just my stuff for an overnight conference! The big duffel bag we carried started out with disposable diapers but was later filled with souvenirs. We also fit in our camera, guidebooks, journals, a little paper, and markers.

The real sacrifice? No toys. Were we *nuts?* We faced hours of train travel (one particular ride was ten hours long) with little to entertain our children but our wits and humor. And we're the family that usually packs a car to the gills with boredom busters, just to keep the kids from whining and fighting. On this trip, we certainly held our breath.

To our delight and astonishment, the kids bickered very little and found many ways to occupy themselves. They checked the guidebooks for sites to see. Calculated exchange rates. Journaled. Snoozed to recharge after charging between trains. Played with baby Elisa—the best toy of all. Stared out the windows at the passing scenery.

We did goofy things, like opening the train windows and letting our hair blow back while we screamed into the wind. Gordy paid the kids *lire* to jog laps through aisles and do chin-ups on the luggage bars. (Aimee wore herself out before discovering how little one thousand *lire* was worth in American pennies.) We cuddled a lot, talked a lot, and played many of the word games in this book. Nevertheless, to be honest, there were huge chunks of time when we all contentedly did nothing. (On trains you eventually enter a zombielike state induced by the gentle rocking from side to side.) I guess you could say we learned to relax. I remember getting to the end of that ten-hour ride and marveling that the kids had done it and stayed so amazingly cheerful.

Oh, come on, you may think with disbelief. *No whining?* Well, yes, some whines did come with the territory. We simply learned to tune the whining out and joke about it. Aimee—who was six—got it in her head that she *had* to have one of the beeping pocket pets sold in the train stations at astronomical prices. It didn't even beep in any interesting foreign languages. I parroted repeatedly, "They will probably be ten dollars at K mart, instead of thirty. Wait until we get to America." Also, Aimee was quite often hungry when the rest of us were not. I thought about making her a T-shirt stating:

I WHINED AND DINED IN SWITZERLAND, ITALY, AND FRANCE!

To boot, Brother was sometimes a tease. He couldn't resist freaking her out by telling her she was walking on gravestones inside a cathedral. "That white stick is really someone's finger bone," he'd smirk. But basically the kids were good company.

Were they really old enough to appreciate the trip? Absolutely. Elisa doesn't remember it. Yet I have frozen in my memory bank an image of that bitsy thing leaning out the window of our guide boat in Venice. She was entranced by a man paddling a gondola, then later by a grandma in the seat next to us who singsonged a nursery poem to her in Italian. It turned out to be a kick having a baby along on that trip. Babies get you attention and lots of *oohs* and *aahs* in various languages. I do admit, however, that age ten months was the perfect window of opportunity, because we didn't have to chase her. Her limited movement—but for her staggering first steps on the trains (she fell down when we walked on land!)—made life easier.

Aimee did not completely appreciate the countless ancient buildings that excited us older folks. Yet judging from her scrapbook, it is apparent that she loved many things on that vacation—the bunk beds in our Swiss hotel, for instance. Her memories are no less important than my own.

Tyler was the perfect age to appreciate the history and architecture of Europe, which he had studied in school. The Colosseum in Rome fascinated him. The thought of people having been sacrificed to lions there (ugh) was just gruesome enough to appeal to a sixth-grade boy. I couldn't count the number of times he saw an enormous cathedral covered with ornate carvings and cried out, "Oh! Cool! Look at *that* one!" I confess that Rome was the only city I found stressful, due to crowds and potential pickpockets, but in the end, it was worth going there simply because my son loved it so much.

Enjoying One Another

One important lesson we learned is that kids can actually learn to live with, and cope with, temporary boredom. Sibling fighting also tends to calm after the first few days of a family vacation of any sort. As kids get older, even elementary-school-aged, they tend to become too peer dependent, even disdainful of younger kids. Consequently, our kids do best when we get out of the house, we break patterns, and they only have each other and us to play with. Little ones gravitate to big ones' laps. Kids find ways to amuse each other. Mom and Dad have countless opportunities for little tickles, big hugs, and conversations of all sizes.

Spontaneity. Flexibility. Simplicity. Playfulness.

Trust in your children's abilities to make fun for themselves—and to make fun for you, too. Escape with your family periodically. Get away from your daily routines. Enjoy your family travels over and over again with enthusiastic, true-adventure stories told around your dinner table—stories told from different points of view, yet forming one cohesive family memory.

minute
fun

PICNIC LIST
Did you play this when you were a kid?

> Mom: "I'm going on a picnic, and I'm taking a . . . watermelon."
> Kid: "I'm going on a picnic, and I'm taking a watermelon and, uh . . . chocolate cake!"
> Keep going, repeating all items previously mentioned until you burn out. If you're burnt out to begin with, have your child describe everything he would pack for a picnic, counting the items on your fingers or writing them down (you can do this for him).

DRESS THE BEAR
Take turns adding clothing (verbally) to an imaginary bear: blue-and-white polka-dotted T-shirt, yellow shorts, purple mittens, etc. The trick is not to repeat clothing items or color combinations. Try to remember the whole outfit later.

TRIP DIARIES
Your roving reporters can use an inexpensive tape recorder and blank tapes, as well as disposable cameras to take pictures as they please. (After use, the whole camera goes to the photo developer.) Budding authors can use a wide-lined pad to write trip impressions and illustrate with drawings, photos, or cutouts from brochures. They can also help keep track of mileage and plan the quickest travel routes.

chapter 15

make memories!

Establishing or Renewing a Playful Home

Break through your misconceptions about play, try something new, and be prepared to enjoy more creative, joy-filled parenting!

K*nock, knock.* I opened the door to find a man about six foot four, in a business suit, carrying a briefcase.

"Would you like to buy some life insurance?" he asked in a teeny, tiny voice. A most peculiar, teeny, tiny head towered atop the crisp white shirt and tie.

"Oh, yes!" I replied. "Please, do come in."

The man entered with a weird, staggering walk. I invited him to have a seat. He stumbled backward into an easy chair, and with awkward exaggeration, he crossed one leg over the other. He giggled.

"Would you like a cup of coffee?" I asked.

"No, thanks," he squeaked. "I feel a little sick."

Suddenly his oddly shaped stomach began to writhe. A growling noise came from inside his pants. Suddenly out of the front of the shirt, near the pants waistline, popped Tyler's head. We unbuttoned the shirt to reveal three-and-a-half-year-old Aimee, sitting atop eight-year-old Tyler's shoulders.

Ah, yes. Just another crazy evening at the Sargent house.

It started with a little silliness and no real plan—Tyler just goofing off, climbing into and being swallowed up by a pair of his dad's pants. We have funny pictures of kids in diapers standing in Dad's shoes, too.

But once Gordy put Aimee on Tyler's shoulders, buttoned a business shirt on her, and tucked it in at the waist, Tyler vanished. The result looked so bizarre, so much like a real man with a child's head, that we all decided to create a Sargent's Funniest Home Video. Various "takes," which we spent the entire fun-filled evening on, culminated in the final version, complete with tie, briefcase, and Aimee's insurance line.

As you learn to play more with your own family, you may find some strange ways to play, as we often do. I guess it takes being on the lookout for those things that have the potential to be funny, and toying with the ideas a bit. Don't be afraid to try something new, even if it is a little weird! Events like the making of our video will stick in our children's minds forever.

CREATING A PLAYFUL CLIMATE

In this book we've covered a wide variety of ways your family might play—from silly play, to adapting table games, to nature hikes. I've offered quick and easy Five-Minute Fun ideas you can play anywhere—in the car, in a doctor's waiting room, at the beach. Yet cultivating a feeling of camaraderie between all the members of your family will require some effort and commitment.

It takes practice to find activities the family can enjoy together, taking age differences, personality differences, and developmental abilities into account. Play between differently aged siblings and adults is often a series of compromises and trades. Sometimes that means letting a little one interrupt the fast pace of a table game to let her take a turn rolling the dice or moving a game piece around the board so she thinks she's playing too.

Getting together as a family will be more desirable for all if you create a climate in your home that's conducive to playfulness. That means avoiding put-downs and unconstructive criticism between all family members—kids and adults alike. Even "constructive," unrelenting criticism can be as irritating as a drippy faucet, driving away feelings of playfulness. I've discovered I have a three-complaint limit, even when the complaints are justified. After about three complaints, I'm always due for some compliments or affection. My children are the same way and have learned to tell me when unrelenting corrections become nagging.

Here are some other ways to make your home a place where playfulness can grow.

"LIGHT UP"

At the end of a day full of toddler messes and limited adult conversation, it's tempting to unload your troubles on a spouse the instant he (or perhaps she, if you're a stay-at-home dad) walks in the door. Yet it's likely the returning parent is hoping to find home an oasis from work worries, a place where his or her presence has been missed. We each want to be seen not only as an extra pair of hands, but as the valuable person we are.

Greet family members as returning heroes instead of yesterday's news. Think about how great it feels to enter a room and have other people's faces light up. When I was newly married, Gary Smalley's timeless book *For Better or for Best*[23] made me aware of the strong impact this can have on a marriage. Small children "light up" spontaneously with their whole bodies as they stampede towards the door, crying out, "Daddy's home!" I try to remember to do the same on occasion, running to the door, saying, "There's my handsome hunk!" or some such thing. Children also yearn to be welcomed home with open arms after a long day at school or a night spent with friends. How much nicer it is for your child, instead of hearing, "Oh, hi. Now run along and clean your bedroom," to hear you excitedly say, "You're home! I'm *so* glad to see you!"

CREATE FAMILY RITUALS

Children often become attached to minirituals we create over the years. Gordy and my girls do a bit from the Three Stooges that involves some very strange hand motions and a few *whoop-whoop*s.

They keep it secret even from me. They like having something special just between them and their daddy.

Children also often enjoy pet names, if they aren't derogatory. (If they say they don't like a name, don't use it again.) Some pet names seem logical—for instance, variations on your child's real name, or words reflecting his or her size ("Peanut," "Half-Pint"). Other nicknames may emerge based on your family lore or even for no apparent reason at all. My kids always loved it when Gordy called them "Hot Dog" when they were little. When friends were over, and he accidentally called someone else Hot Dog, I heard plaintive cries: "No, I'm the Hot Dog! He's the Hamburger." Go figure!

Other rituals may develop from a wacky combination of kisses and hugs. For instance, we give our kids three of each every night. These are great ways to nurture your relationship with your children and create special memories that will last a lifetime.

On a grander scale, rituals can become traditions. On most birthdays in our family, we deck out the table with a special birthday tablecloth. And—at least for a moment—the guest of honor dons a special, colorful birthday beanie that looks a bit like a jester's hat. We also like to waken the birthday child with a lit candle stuck in a piece of toast, while singing "Happy Birthday." We make it a point to watch old videos of the birthday child one evening during his or her birthday week.

Use your imagination to come up with new, creative, parent-child rituals or family traditions of your own.

CLING TO PREDICTABLE FAMILY TIMES

Doing things together with all family members present will help your children see your whole family as a single unit. Try to create some predictable daily and weekly family times, and tell your kids that you need those times so you can all stay connected. Exactly how you do this is up to you.

For us, our sacred times are dinnertimes and weekly church times. Certainly our kids complain sometimes about having to drag themselves away from playmates to be home every day at 6:30 for family dinner, and having to drag themselves out of bed for church every Sunday. We do make exceptions on occasion, even for the whole family, perhaps taking a Sunday hike. And in the long, lazy days of summer, it can be hard to gather the troops for dinner so early in the evening.

But it helps us to have these times often, and everyone usually shows up without argument unless they've made previous arrangements. It's become such a routine that if anyone is missing, it feels awkward.

Getting everyone together won't guarantee *quality* time, of course. Often getting everyone in the car on time leads to bickering. But when we're aware that's happening, we try to turn our vehicle into more of a party car. Gordy turns up the stereo full blast with music we all enjoy, and we all sing along. Once, Aimee brought a joke book and read us jokes in the car during a fifteen-minute drive.

After church, Gordy and I often hunger for a bit more family time, so we'll squeeze in at least another hour by taking the kids to a Mexican restaurant before we hit home and scatter to the four winds. I also encourage this "tradition" so I can get out of cooking lunch, of course!

DINNER PLAY

What? Eating meals together doesn't sound like play to you? Well, surely you've made worms out of straw paper covers, haven't you? (Gently scrunch the paper down to the end of the straw before pulling it off. Lay it on the table and drip a few drops of liquid on it to watch it wiggle.) And have you tried playing tic-tac-toe with sugar and artificial-sweetener packets?

My favorite dinner toy is a fork that looks like a real one but telescopes out to about three feet long. You can eat with it normally for a while. Then you can hide it under the table to extend it, and surprise someone by reaching across the table to their plate, casually asking, "May I have a bite of yours?" Elisa loves to surprise company with it.

Of course, we always try to have a reverent moment of prayer first. Praying for each other's needs is a great way to keep the kids involved in each other's lives and show concern for each other. There are times, however, when a five-year-old's prayers fervently and endlessly cover every ache and pain in our household, plus those of extended relatives. I confess to sitting with one eye closed and the other peeking longingly at my quickly cooling food. Eventually, the one who is most hungry interrupts with a gentle "Amen!"

We do care about table manners too, and we generally try to encourage good ones. But beware of spending more mealtime energy keeping elbows off the table than finding out about your children's days. Family meals can be one of the best ways to draw close as a family and get to know each other better.

KEEP YOUR MEMORIES ALIVE

To remember all your great times together as a family, get in the habit of recording them somehow. Take photographs or videos, or jot down what you did in a diary or even on a Post-it note. Keep your camera handy with plenty of film, and if you have a video camera (a great investment), keep the battery charged.

Look at your keepsakes on occasion, and talk about them— perhaps this summer, when you make a scrapbook. Add mementos from the past school year. Tell and retell your children funny stories about themselves. Relive the fun.

PLAY ON!

In this book we've explored many different barriers to play. I hope we've touched on some that affect you personally. I also hope that some solutions we've talked about have proven useful to you. Perhaps you've learned to use toys or games in new, fun ways or have been inspired to get out and explore your neighborhood a bit more. It may be that you're anticipating your next great family adventure, or you've decided to simplify your life and enjoy a little silliness at home. I hope, above all, you've been inspired to play more often and to make the most of this precious time with your children!

If that's the case or you have ideas you'd like to share with other parents, I'd enjoy hearing from you. You can reach me through my Web site at http://www.parentchildplay.com. The site offers lists of great resources and links to others to help encourage you in your parenting adventure. Ready? Set? Go and make some new, playful memories!

5 minute fun

BLANKET FORT

Don't forget to join the fun when your little one wants to make a blanket fort or village in your living room! Move a little furniture around, and use lots of sheets (easy to fold again later). Stick on a construction-paper doorbell. Get the plasticware and have a pretend tea party with stuffed animals, or lie on the floor in your fort under the dining-room table and look at the posters you've taped under there! Or be a monster, attacking the outside of the fort while the defenders giggle.

COMPUTER DIARY

To remember more about what your child was like at each age and stage, keep an ongoing diary in the computer. Update it at least once every year or two, but when your child's a little tot, you may want to add something every few months. A written diary will do as well. However, if it's in the computer, you can't misplace it. You can print copies later for yourself, long-distance relatives, and your child—to show his own children someday!

Address it to your child. "Dear Adam. Today you are eighteen months old! You love to bang on your xylophone and to put on that little plastic duck nose and quack like a duck. You are so funny!"

"Here are some of your new words: . . ." (or funny sentences). Write out what your child says as he pronounces it phonetically. Also add notes about incidents that reveal how your child thinks or demonstrates personality traits. Does your mind go blank when you finally have time to write in your diary? As events occur, jot them on the borders of the calendar hanging on your fridge. At the end of the year, copy those notes into your diary before you throw out the calendar. You can print tidbits from your file to put next to photos in photo albums too.

appendix

Books

Choices Are Not Child's Play: Helping Your Kids Make Wise Decisions by Pat Holt and Grace Ketterman (Harold Shaw Publishers, 1990).

Don't Give In, Give Choices: Winning Your Child's Cooperation by Pat Holt and Grace Ketterman (Harold Shaw Publishers, 1997).

The Five Love Languages of Children by Gary Chapman and Ross Campbell (Northfield Publishers, 1997).

The Five Love Languages of Teenagers by Gary Chapman and Ross Campbell (Northfield Publishers, 2001).

For Better or for Best by Gary Smalley (Zondervan Publishing House, 1996).

If Only He Knew by Gary Smalley (Zondervan Publishing House, 1997).

Megaskills: Building Children's Achievement for the Information Age by Dorothy Rich (Mariner Books, 1998).

Megaskills: In School and in Life—The Best Gift You Can Give Your Child by Dorothy Rich (Houghton Mifflin Company, 1992).

Once-a-Month Cooking by Mary Beth Lagerborg and Mimi Wilson (Broadman and Holman, 1999).

Raising Your Spirited Child by Mary Sheedy Kurcinka (Harper Perennial, 1992).

The Way They Learn by Cynthia Ulrich Tobias (Focus on the Family, 1998).

When You Feel Like Screaming by Pat Holt, Grace Ketterman, and Jo Kadlecek (Harold Shaw Publishers, 2001).

You Can't Make Me (But I Can Be Persuaded) by Cynthia Ulrich Tobias (Waterbrook Press, 1999).

Children's Books

The Little Mouse, the Red Ripe Strawberry, and the Big Hungry Bear by Don and Audrey Wood (Child's Play International, 1998, 2001).

The Treasure Tree: Helping Kids Get Along and Enjoy Each Other by John and Cindy Trent and Gary and Norma Smalley; illustrated by Judy Love (Thomas Nelson, 1998).

The Two Trails: A Treasure Tree Adventure by John Trent; illustrated by Judy Love (Thomas Nelson, 1997).

We're Going on a Bear Hunt by Michael Rosen and Helen Oxenbury (Little Simon, Classic Board Books, 1997).

Counseling Services

The Center for Counseling and Health Resources, Inc.
547 Dayton
Edmonds, WA 98020

1-888-771-5166
www.aplaceofhope.com

Dr. Gregory L. Jantz, who has a Ph. D. in counseling psychology, directs The Center, a state-licensed mental-health facility, with mental-health, medical, and chemical-dependency counselors at three locations in Washington state, plus a clinic in Quito, Ecuador. Jantz authored *Healing the Scars of Emotional Abuse* (Fleming H. Revell, 1995) and ten other books on topics including eating disorders. Michael A. Weiford, a licensed independent clinical social worker, is The Center's mental-health program director.

National Domestic Violence Hotline
1-800-799-SAFE
http://www.ndvh.org

Additional Parenting Resources

Laurie Winslow Sargent's Web site: www.parentchildplay.com

index of activities

questions for reflection

(For individual use or group discussion)

Chapter 1: One-Size-Fits-All?

1. Consider the variety of ways you can play with your child. What new way can you play with your child this week?

2. Has your child surprised you in some way recently? For instance, have you been intrigued by the way he defined something or how he played with a toy in a way you hadn't thought of? Jot it down to share with him when he is older.

3. Did this chapter help you see how you might develop more of a playful attitude rather than a goal-oriented focus on specific activities? In what way? In what areas might you need to loosen up a little?

4. Have you ever been surprised by the depth of your emotions toward your child in the course of play, as I was in the invisible-cookie story? Write down that experience.

Chapter 2: What Gets in the Way?

1. Think of a time when a playtime turned to tears or frustration for you or your child. Write down any barriers that might have interfered with that particular playtime: age differences, personality differences, sibling rivalry, etc.

2. How playful do you feel in general, and how easy do you find spontaneous play? In what ways could you add some spontaneity to your life?

3. Do you recognize any clusters of barriers that habitually

get in the way for you? Are they mostly related to time and energy limits, uncertainty about activity choices, lack of motivation or joy, or family stress?

Chapter 3: Why Try?

1. Consider the five benefits of play: teaching, building self-esteem, intimacy, joy, and a grasp of broader concepts. Can you recall a time when you taught your child something new while playing together?

2. Have you seen your child apply what you've taught him to other activities?

3. Can you recall a time when you said or did something that obviously boosted your child's self-esteem? a time when she boosted yours? What were you doing together at the time?

4. Can you remember a joyful or funny moment that occurred while you were playing with your child? Share that experience with at least one other person and write it down so you can remember and enjoy it years from now.

Chapter 4: Derailing Tantrums and Defiance

1. Think about the last time your child behaved negatively—whining, fighting with siblings, throwing a tantrum, or refusing to comply with rules. Could his behavior have been caused by his need for attention?

2. Talk to your child and come up with some ways he can ask for attention in a more direct way.

3. Can you see a correlation between consistency in discipline and your own ability to feel playful? Is it possible to be more consistent with discipline, yet spend *less* time and energy controlling your kids, giving you more time to have fun together?

4. Considering your child's physical and emotional needs, list some ways you can better anticipate those needs to help prevent or defuse battles or emotional meltdowns.

Chapter 5: Maybe Later, Dear

1. What tasks drain your time and energy the most? Are most of these necessary? (For example, a new baby, sick relatives, working outside the home to support the family.) If you find that the most draining tasks are indeed necessary, make a commitment to have some compassion on yourself and ask for help from others when you need it.

2. If you have a physical limitation on your energy level right now—pregnancy, a long-term illness, or some other affliction—is there a way you can increase your child's independence so you can reserve more energy to play with him? What fun activities can you do with your child that still give you the rest you need?

3. Does much of the busyness in your life come from activities you have chosen? That might include volunteer work (PTA, church, politics) or outside work done to earn money for luxuries or keep careers on track. Can you give up any activities for now, so that you might enjoy your children while they are small?

Chapter 6: Pampers to Proms and Beyond

1. Are you surprised to discover how early you can play and have fun with a baby?

2. Can you think of anything your toddler has done that at first seemed just messy, strange, or frustrating, but did indeed have some logic behind it and revealed something your child has learned?

3. Can you think of anything funny your preschooler said that revealed something interesting about the way a kid thinks at his age? Share that with another parent. Has your child done anything that surprised and delighted you because you thought he was too young to do it yet?

4. Can you see how playfulness can be carried on into adulthood? Try being playful with your spouse or a friend this week.

Chapter 7: But We're So Different!

1. What makes your child(ren) unique? Do you see personality traits in your child now that you became aware of when he was much younger—even as a baby?

2. What traits do you have the most difficulty with? Is that because your own personality is similar or different?

3. Have any of the temperamental traits we've discussed affected a specific time when you played with your kids or how you reacted to them? How can you adjust activities to make them more successful?

4. Think of ways your child's inborn traits might eventually benefit him or her as an adult. Can you learn to appreciate him more and to be more tolerant of the way he is created?

Chapter 8: I Don't Feel like Playing

1. Think of some ways to make play less frustrating or boring. Talk with other parents about this to get some ideas.

2. Do you think the way you were raised affects the way you play with your children? Do you think it is possible to change that? Try some of the solutions in this chapter.

3. Do you think the ability to be playful with children, and in life in general, is a personality trait, a gift, or a learned skill? If it's a skill, where might you learn and practice it?

4. Is there something new you could try (for example, reading humorous books, taking a class, or joining a group) that could begin stretching you emotionally?

Chapter 9: What Else Is Happening under My Roof?

1. What family stresses are you currently experiencing?

2. How is your stress affecting your playfulness with your child and your relationship with him overall? Is it causing you to withdraw from him or snap at him more easily? How perceptive of that stress do you think your child is? Consider talking about

it directly with him and allowing him to express his feelings about it.

3. Is that stress temporary (even up to a year) or long-term? Does it have the potential to continue throughout your child's childhood?

4. Are you able to go through the motions of play? Is your child still benefiting somehow, despite your current lack of physical endurance or emotional investment? Is your child commenting on your lack of playfulness, or is he happy to have you simply set aside time to be with him?

Chapter 10: Chores Are Done, Time for Fun!

1. Is it possible to be firm enough to have your children respect you and listen to you, but to be playful as well?

2. In what ways can you help your child become more independent, self-reliant, responsible, and helpful in order to help create more time, energy, and motivation for play?

3. Can you see some of the potential long-term effects you can have on your child by nurturing responsibility in him right now?

4. This week, find some new way to nurture helpfulness in your child through play. That may mean slowing down to let him "help" you with a task.

Chapter 11: Find the Best, Chuck the Rest!

1. Have you ever struggled with boredom or impatience while playing with toys with your child? Try some of the tips in this chapter to adapt games or toys you own so you can have more fun together.

2. Consider the toys you have purchased or are considering buying for your child, and whether they do or don't have long-term play value based on the list in this chapter. Have you ever pushed your child to use toys he owns, despite the fact that they aren't much fun, simply because of what they cost you or a relative, or because of their supposed educational value? If you

can't adapt them to make them more fun, someone else may love finding them at your garage sale!

3. The next time your child wants you to buy something with limited play value, can you say no more confidently? If he insists, try using The List, so he can learn to prioritize.

4. Have you ever given your child the opportunity to earn play materials as rewards for reaching his personal goals? Help your child develop a plan to *earn* his next toy.

5. Can you find one new way to store your child's play materials so they will be more useful, your child will play with them longer, and your frustration with clutter will decrease?

Chapter 12: ABC and Do-Re-Mi

1. How can you integrate play into teaching your child? (For example, teaching phonics through fun word games.)

2. Do you have confidence in your own ability to teach your child or to learn how? Learn something new together this week, perhaps through library books or at a museum.

3. Look around your home for tools you can use spontaneously to teach your child. Consider purchasing a few new things. You can find placemats with interesting things on them—for instance, the alphabet in Braille or sign language, or a map of the United States, which make for impromptu dinner-table learning. Don't ignore traditional games like Monopoly, which teach math and reading skills.

Chapter 13: Time to Get Out! Or Stay In?

1. Do you feel the need to stay in for a change, having been so busy that you need some downtime with your child? Can you use what you learned in the time and energy chapter to be selective about your activities—even those you do with your children? Do something simple together today.

2. If you're home with the kids more than you'd like to be, what is keeping you from getting out? Are those things truly

insurmountable? Pick up your phone or go on-line to find out what's available in your area.

3. If you've felt isolated, can you make a renewed effort to find other parents who may also feel isolated?

4. If you're overwhelmed by the thought of getting out of the house with small children, yet you want to devote an hour to one child and his special interests, can you find someone willing to watch his sibling(s)? Would you be willing to do the same for another parent?

5. Practice getting out more with all your kids, even to do something very simple like taking walks together. This will help you develop routines so getting out goes more smoothly.

Chapter 14: Playing Far from Home

1. Can you see the variety of ways you and your family can vacation together? List the types of trips that appeal to you and others in your family.

2. When will you have your next family adventure? Begin thinking now about that and planning time for it. Where might you go? How will you save money for it?

3. On your next family vacation, think of ways to keep it simple. Strive for more spontaneity, flexibility, and playfulness as you travel. Trust your children's abilities to entertain themselves without a lot of toys.

Chapter 15: Make Memories!

1. Can you keep your eyes open to things that are potentially funny? Be willing to drop your chores and take time for some spontaneous fun, like creating a goofy home video or having a water fight.

2. What can you do to create a more playful climate in your home? Will it help to show more appreciation for those in your family? Try to "light up" the next time your child or spouse walks in the door, and sandwich corrections with praise and hugs.

3. Do you have any special family rituals or pet names? Think of something new you can try, like buying a special birthday hat.

4. Make sure you have some predictable, sacred family times, when all family members must be present and accounted for. If your kids gripe about those times, can you find ways to make them more fun and explain to your kids the need for family time?

5. How can you keep your memories of fun family times alive? Set aside time to look at old photos or videos together. Perhaps the only trip you need this summer is a trip down memory lane, looking at keepsakes from previous adventures. Get as much mileage out of your family fun as you can!

endnotes

Chapter 1: One-Size-Fits-All?

[1] *New World Dictionaries* (Paramus, N.J.: Prentice Hall Press, 1971).

[2] *Webster's New World Thesaurus,* Revised Edition (New York: Simon and Schuster, 1985).

[3] Frank J. Myers and Gary Baker, "I Swear," copyright © 1994 Morgan-Active Songs, Inc.

[4] Arthur Kraft, *Are You Listening to Your Child? How to Bridge the Communication Gap Through Creative Play Sessions* (New York: Walker & Co., 1973).

Chapter 3: Why Try?

[5] T. Berry Brazelton, author of *The Irreducible Needs of Children,* quoted by the *New York Times,* 14 November 2000.

[6] Proverbs 15:13

Chapter 4: Derailing Tantrums and Defiance

[7] Pat Holt and Grace Ketterman, *Choices Are Not Child's Play: Helping Your Kids Make Wise Decisions* (Wheaton, Ill.:Harold Shaw Publishers, 1990).

Chapter 5: Maybe Later, Dear

[8] Originally published in *Christian Parenting Today*; reprinted in *Life in Our House* flip calendar (Bloomington, Minn.: Garborg's Heart 'n Home, 1994).

Chapter 6: Pampers to Proms and Beyond

[9] "What Grown-Ups Understand about Child Development: A National Benchmark Survey" was sponsored by three organizations dedicated to the welfare of young children: CIVITAS Initiative, ZERO TO THREE, and BRIO Corporation. Researched by DYG, Inc. Results released Oct. 2000.

[10] J. Madeleine Nash, "Special Report: Fertile Minds," *Time,* 149, no. 5 (3 February 1997). See <http://www.time.com/time/magazine/1997/dom/97203/cover0.html>.

[11] If your child's motor skills are significantly delayed, you may also see delays in speech, understanding, and your child's ability to dress and feed himself or socialize with other children. If you have concerns, ask your pediatrician to do a developmental assessment on your child—not just a checkup for illnesses or immunizations. Your child may be referred to a developmental pediatrician or clinic, or to the special services department of your public school for further testing and treatment options.

[12] Mercer Mayer, *When I Get Bigger* (New York: Random House, 1999).

Chapter 7: But We're So Different!

13 Stella Chess and Alexander Thomas, *Know Your Child: An Authoritative Guide For Today's Parents* (New York: Basic Books, 1987), 31. Although this book is out of print, the authors' methods for classifying temperamental traits have been quoted in countless other books on this topic.

14 Mary Sheedy Kurcinka, *Raising Your Spirited Child: A Guide for Parents Whose Child Is More Intense, Sensitive, Perceptive, Persistent, or Energetic* (New York: Harper Perrenial, 1992). This book and an accompanying workbook offer tips for helping get through day-to-day tasks when strong temperamental traits can get in the way.

Chapter 8: I Don't Feel like Playing

15 Adele Faber and Elaine Mazlish, *Siblings Without Rivalry: How to Help Your Children Live Together So You Can Live Too* (New York: W. W. Norton and Company, 1987).

16 Gregory L. Jantz, *Healing the Scars of Emotional Abuse* (Grand Rapids, Mich.: Fleming H. Revell, 1995), 86. Jantz is the founder and Executive Director of The Center for Counseling and Resources, Inc., in Edmonds, Wash.

Chapter 9: What Else Is Happening under My Roof?

17 Faith Hickman Brynie, *101 Questions about Your Immune System* (Breckenridge, Colo.: Twenty First Century Books, 2000). References to T. H. Holmes and R. H. Rahe, "The Social Re-Adjustment Rating Scale," *Journal of Psychosomatic Research*, 11 (1967), 213–218.

18 Dr. Seuss, *The Cat in the Hat* (New York: Random House, 1957), 16, 18.

19 Review chapter 5 to find activities you might eliminate during your time of stress.

20 If you are in a situation like this, call your domestic violence hot line to talk through your options with a counselor.

21 Sam McBratney, *Guess How Much I Love You* (Cambridge, Mass.: Candlewick Press, 1994).

Chapter 10: Chores Are Done, Time for Fun!

22 Dorothy Rich, *MegaSkills* (Boston: Houghton Mifflin Company, 1992), 52.

Chapter 15: Make Memories!

23 Gary Smalley, *For Better or for Best* (Grand Rapids, Mich.: Zondervan Publishing House, 1996).

Portions of this book, including "Independent Play" and "Grown-Up Games Made Easy," were previously published by *Christian Parenting Today* magazine with David C. Cook Publishing Co.